Selah

A Revision of
Psalms, Hymns and Spiritual Songs

Selah
A Guide to Music in the Bible

A Revision of
*Psalms, Hymns
and Spiritual Songs*

Donald Thiessen

Cornerstone Press Chicago
Chicago, Illinois

Scripture taken from the New American Standard Bible, ©1960, 1962 1963, 1968, 1971, 1972, 1973, 1975, 1977 by The Lockman Foundation. Used by permission.

Cornerstone Press Chicago
939 W. Wilson Ave.
Chicago, IL 60640
www.cornerstonepress.com
cspress@jpusa.org
© 2002 by Donald Thiessen
All rights reserved. First edition 1993
Revised edition 2002

Cover and book design by Hugo Thysse

ISBN 0-940895-47-1
Printed in the United States of America
07 06 05 04 03 02   5 4 3 2 1

Library of Congress Cataloging-in-Publication Data

Thiessen, Donald
  Selah : a guide to music in the Bible / Donald Thiessen.–3rd ed.
      p. cm.
Rev. ed. of: Psalms, hymns, and spiritual songs. 2nd ed. c1994.
"Scripture taken from the New American Standard Bible"–T.p. verso
ISBN 0-940895-47-1 (pbk. : alk. paper)
  1. Music in the Bible. I. Thiessen, Donald. Psalms, hymns, and
spiritual songs. II. Bible. English. New American Standard. III. Title.
  ML166 .T45 2002
  220.8'78–dc21
                                                        2002002259

Contents

Foreword	viii
Preface	ix
Introduction	x
Explanation of General Format	xi

Part One: Bible Passages

BOOKS OF THE OLD TESTAMENT

Genesis	1
Exodus	3
Leviticus	7
Numbers	8
Deuteronomy	11
Joshua	13
Judges	15
Ruth	19
First Samuel	19
Second Samuel	24
First Kings	29
Second Kings	31
First Chronicles	33
Second Chronicles	43
Ezra	50
Nehemiah	52
Esther	57
Job	57
Psalms	60
Proverbs	87
Ecclesiastes	88
Song of Solomon	89
Isaiah	89
Jeremiah	96
Lamentations	99
Ezekiel	99
Daniel	101
Hosea	103
Joel	104
Amos	105
Obadiah	107

Jonah	107
Micah	107
Nahum	107
Habakkuk	107
Zephaniah	109
Haggai	109
Zechariah	109
Malachi	110

BOOKS OF THE NEW TESTAMENT

The Gospel:	
According to Matthew	113
According to Mark	115
According to Luke	115
According to John	116
Acts	116
Romans	117
First Corinthians	118
Second Corinthians	119
Galatians	119
Ephesians	119
Philippians	121
Colossians	121
First Thessalonians	121
Second Thessalonians	122
First Timothy	122
Second Timothy	122
Titus	122
Philemon	122
Hebrews	122
James	123
First Peter	124
Second Peter	124
First John	124
Second John	124
Third John	124
Jude	124
Revelation	124

Part Two: Topical Concordance	130
Hebrew Concordance	156
Greek Concordance	164

Foreword

I have long been a fan of anyone who truly loves the Christian musician. Having chatted with the author/compiler of this book on several occasions, I am assured of his honest concern for those embarking on the musician's journey. Too few understand or take the time to work through the questions that serious Christian musicians must find solutions to if they want to serve God with their skill.

In this book Dr. Don Thiessen has provided the foundation for what we must do. God's Word is the essential source for our faith and practice. It is therefore with thanks to the Lord and to Dr. Thiessen that we gladly offer this help to all who are concerned about pleasing the Lord with their musical efforts. In the words of A. W. Tozer, "Nothing less than a whole Bible will make a whole Christian." If that be true, it is no less true with regard to those verses that clearly, contextually speak to this issue in the Scriptures. Studying the Bible's own words about music is central to developing a mature theology of music. Alas, after nearly two thousand years the Church still is in want of one!

It has now been several years since we were privileged to publish *Psalms, Hymns and Spiritual Songs*. You presently hold what is, in my view, a genuine improvement of the original manuscript! We each may agree or disagree with Dr. Theissen's various points of added commentary in *Selah*, but I trust all will be stirred to deeper thought and serious study of music in the Word of God, "the only perfect rule for faith, doctrine and practice." That is our joyful prayer...and song! May this book bring the truth of God's commentary about music and its use ever more into the hearts, minds, and lives of His servants.

In Jesus,
GLENN KAISER

Preface to the Third Edition

When the first edition of this work had sold out after a few years, I thought the book had had a reasonable life and ministry. I had gone on to other pursuits with less involvement in music than previously. I did receive encouragement, however, to consider a new edition that would include commentary on the passages to take readers to a bit more thought and reflection on some of the issues of contemporary music. The exercise of working my way through the Scriptures was excellent for me, and I hope that it will be for many others.

When one writes a book, the moment arrives when it's time to consider it done. There is always more that could be added to improve the book. The more one studies a subject, the more one becomes aware of one's inadequacies. That is certainly the case with this book as well. Far more could be said about some of the concepts, but I present this as my offering to you today. It might set someone else in a direction to provide what I haven't. Or someday I might take the study to another, deeper level.

I pray that this study will inspire others to serve the Church in music or in the other arts. God loves beauty as evidenced by all the beauty He has created. We need to offer our creations of beauty to Him as an act of worship. That is when music, and all art, function at their ultimate.

Introduction

Music continues to be a catalyst in many of the "worship wars" being waged in our churches, as Christians seek to minister to each other and the pre-Christian community around them. Too often we try to advocate or defend a particular approach or style apart from what the Scriptures say. It is disconcerting to some that the Scriptures give so little prescriptive instruction on the style and function of music for the people of God. Much of the discussion on music in the Bible is general in nature or simply descriptive as the history of a people is told. Although this gives much freedom to make music in the Church, to have no restrictions is often too constricting for us.

This book is the result of my personal journey to come to terms with this ambiguity. The commentary has been added in an attempt to interact with the text without violating the intention of the writer. When one is passionate about something, the temptation is great to force an opinion on the text that was not intended by the writer. I have attempted to avoid that. With the addition of the Hebrew and Greek concordance, an academic-technical component has been added for those who have an interest in that direction. The commentary, however, is more reflective and instructive in its approach. My hope is that it will help you in your personal journey and as you seek to be effective in ministry.

DON THIESSEN

Explanation of General Format

—quotation marks are used in the text in accordance with modern English usage.

—punctuation changes have been made to conform with modern practice.

—"thou," "thy," and "thee" are changed to "you" except in the language of prayer when addressing Deity.

—personal pronouns are capitalized when pertaining to Deity.

—in keeping with the usage of the New American Standard Bible, the proper name of God in the Old Testament (YHWH) is translated and printed LORD.

—italics are used in the text to indicate words not found in the original Hebrew or Greek but implied by it.

—verbs marked with an asterisk (*) represent historical presents in the Greek which have been translated with an English past tense in order to conform to modern usage.

Part One:
Bible Passages

OLD TESTAMENT

Genesis

Lamech's Offspring 4:19-24

21 And his brother's name was Jubal; he was the father of all those who play the lyre and pipe.

To be first is no small thing. Whether the task is to invent a safety pin or a computer, what is always required is for someone to think of a concept first. Jubal is credited with being the father of all those who play the lyre and harp, that is, those who built and played musical instruments. Being "made in the image of God" includes the capacity for creativity. Music, of course, is one of the creative endeavors that involves the discovery of the properties of sound, the limits of which seem to extend like the capricious "carrot" that never quite reveals its full potential. Where at first, for thousands of years, musicians were limited to natural materials in building their instruments, we now utilize synthetic products that provide sounds we never imagined just decades ago. This continuing discovery of the potential of God's creation will presumably continue and be limited only by our imagination and energy, and for that matter, God's infinite creation.

In this particular passage two instruments are mentioned: the lyre and pipe. The Hebrew word used here and translated *lyre* is *kinnor* (more commonly translated as *harp*), representing some type of stringed instrument of which, apparently, there were several in the ancient world. Whether this specific instrument was lutelike, guitarlike, or harplike is not definitely ascertainable, but by this time the people had obviously discovered that strings of varying lengths, thicknesses, and tensions provided different pitches. The development of stringed instruments as we know them had their beginning with Jubal.

The pipe (*uggab*), then, is the predecessor to all our wind instruments. This might compare to our present panpipe with its combination of pipes of varying lengths to provide a scale, making melody possible. This is also the principle on which the pipe organ works. Or it might have been a flutelike instrument consisting of one pipe with several holes to again make melody possible. On the other hand, the contemporary brass instruments utilize the natural harmonic series of a simple pipe. Which was it? We can only study the meager historical evidence and surmise as to which is likely. From the evidence it is unlikely that this was the precursor of our present-day brass instruments and more likely was the beginnings of our present-day woodwind instruments.

Jacob Fleeing from Laban 31:22-32
27 "Why did you flee secretly and deceive me, and did not tell me, so that I might have sent you away with joy and with songs, with timbrel and with lyre;

Was he truthful? What father sends his child (from the bottom of his heart) away with joy, songs, timbrel, and lyre? But then, Rachel was also deceitful. Had she learned from her husband and her father? The history of both is strewn with incidents of duplicity, deceit, and dishonesty. Possibly Laban was simply reaping what he had sown, just as Jacob did. But all of this was connected to music, which should have accompanied a joyful family celebration. Here, it would have been a farewell party, a celebration of family and prosperity.

In this passage we come across the first reference to a percussion instrument, in this translation, *timbrel*. The Hebrew, *toph*, also has been variously translated as *tabret, tabor,* and *tambourine,* all of which are essentially the same instrument. So already in Genesis at least three of the present-day instrumental families, wind, string, and percussion, have been introduced to us.

Exodus

Red Sea Celebration 15:1-21

1 Then Moses and the sons of Israel sang this song to the LORD, and said,

> "I will sing to the LORD, for He is highly exalted;
> The horse and its rider He has hurled into the sea.
> **2** "The LORD is my strength and song,
> And He has become my salvation;
> This is my God, and I will praise Him;
> My father's God, and I will extol Him.

20 And Miriam the prophetess, Aaron's sister, took the timbrel in her hand, and all the women went out after her with timbrels and with dancing.

21 And Miriam answered them, "Sing to the LORD, for He is highly exalted; The horse and his rider He has hurled into the sea."

It could be argued that this is an example of antiphonal choral music in which the men formed a choir to which the women then responded. They did, however, not respond only in words but with timbrel (*toph*) and dancing (*mecholah*). It was Miriam who responds in what might have been a refrain sung as the women danced. The singing (*shir*), dancing (not to be confused with modern dance), and instruments combined to be the vehicle for a celebration of deliverance for several million or more people who were finally free after four hundred years of slavery.

This, the first song (*shirah*) in the Bible, is a poem filled with word pictures. It is an extremely vivid expression of who God is and what He did to save the Israelites. This song never questions who won the battle: it was God the warrior. The destruction of the enemy is described with images:

"went down into the depths like a stone"

"shatters the enemy"

Exodus

"consumes them as chaff"
"the blast of Thy nostrils"
"waters stood up like a heap"
"They sank like lead"
"The earth swallowed them up"
"All the inhabitants of Canaan have melted away"
"they are motionless as stone"

These images combine to provide a powerful description of a deliverance that could only have come from God. These figures of speech combine to paint a powerful picture of the complete defeat of the Egyptian forces.

Giving of the Commandments 19:10-20

13 'No hand shall touch him, but he shall surely be stoned or shot through; whether beast or man, he shall not live.' When the ram's horn sounds a long blast, they shall come up to the mountain."

16 So it came about on the third day, when it was morning, that there were thunder and lightning flashes and a thick cloud upon the mountain and a very loud trumpet sound, so that all the people who *were* in the camp trembled.

19 When the sound of the trumpet grew louder and louder, Moses spoke and God answered him with thunder.

20:1-26

18 And all the people perceived the thunder and the lightning flashes and the sound of the trumpet and the mountain smoking; and when the people saw *it*, they trembled and stood at a distance.

Another new instrument, *yobhel*, is introduced in verse 13. Although it is here translated as "ram's horn," it is not necessarily a different instrument than *shofar* in verse 16. Whether it meant that the instrument was made of a horn or was in the crooked shape of a horn is not at all certain. This is, however, a

Exodus

wind instrument more closely identified with our brass instruments than with the woodwinds because of the embouchure required to produce the sound. The blast (*mashak*) of an instrument as described in verse 13 occurs in only one other passage, Joshua 6:5. The literal meaning of this Hebrew term is "to draw, to drag."

One thing is not clear from a reading of this passage: "Who was blowing the trumpet?" God indicated to Moses that when they heard the sound of the trumpet, they were all to assemble at the mountain. From the account, it seems quite possible that the sound of the trumpet, as was the sound of the thunder and the visible manifestations, was being produced by God, not humans.

God certainly was into sensory experiences when He communicated with His people on this occasion. There was no doubt that God had something to say and there was going to be no excuse from the people that He hadn't warned them. Note all the appeals to the senses in the preparation for and in the giving of the commandments:

SIGHT a mountain they were not to touch
clean clothes
a thick cloud
smoke
fire
lightning flashed
people trembling

    SOUND the blast from the ram's horn
a very loud trumpet sound
thunder
Moses speaking
the Lord speaking

Exodus

> SMELL freshly washed clothing
> smoke
>
> FEEL trembling
> the violently quaking mountain
>
> TASTE (maybe)

Why all the drama? Why not just send the tablets, let us read them, and be done with it? The answer is given in 20:18ff. The people beg to have Moses rather than God speak to them because they fear death if God continues to speak to them. Moses answer is, "Do not be afraid; for God has come in order to test you, and in order that the fear of Him may remain with you, *so that you may not sin*" (italics mine). Why this sensory blitz? The fear of Him, coupled with these instructions, is to keep them, and us, from sin. Will reading this do this? That is God's intention.

The Golden Calf 32:15-20

18 But he said,

> "It is not the sound of the cry of triumph,
> Nor is it the sound of the cry of defeat;
> But the sound of singing I hear."

19 And it came about, as soon as Moses came near the camp, that he saw the calf and *the* dancing; and Moses' anger burned, and he threw the tablets from his hands and shattered them at the foot of the mountain.

There was, apparently, an obvious difference between the sounds *(qol)* of battle and the sounds of worship. Moses, from a distance, was able to distinguish the sound as one of singing and, as he neared the scene, responded in a passionate act of anger: he smashed the tablets that had been presented to the people in such a grand display of nature drama.

Music and dancing *(mecholah),* which had been employed in family events to express joy and in the exodus as an expression of thanksgiving for God's deliverance, has now been turned into a vehicle for worshipping an idol, an abomination before the Lord. Very early in the history of the Israelites, all of God's creation had been desecrated by misuse *(sin).*

Today it is no different. These wonderful, creative expressions are still being used as tools of Satan to mislead his followers and sometimes even the followers of Christ. That, however, must never stop us from using these amazing gifts of creativity from God to praise Him as only His children can.

Leviticus

A Call to Remember 23:24-25

24 "Speak to the sons of Israel, saying, 'In the seventh month on the first of the month, you shall have a rest, a reminder by blowing *of trumpets,* a holy convocation.

The trumpet, or possibly more often the bugle, is still being used to remind. It is most commonly in use in the military, where its sharp, brilliant sound demands the attention of all involved in a particular event. Whether it's a reveille, a review, a march, a ceremony, a funeral, or any other military event, the bugle's distinctive sound demands attention.

When a particular melody is played, a particular response is expected. Here a rest, a holy convocation was expected. Paul relates to this event when in 2 Corinthians 14:8 he indicates that our prophesying needs to be clear and understandable, just like a bugle needs to have a distinct sound for soldiers to understand that they are expected in battle.

Leviticus-Numbers

Music can call us to remember even when there are no words, simply because we associate certain sounds with certain events and ideas. When the bugler played to remind the people about this rest, he will have played the same melody each time. At the sound of that melody all will have responded in the appropriate way. Even the children, growing up and hearing this, will have known the meaning of the music.

Announcement of the Jubilee 25:8-12

9 'You shall then sound a ram's horn abroad on the tenth day of the seventh month; on the day of atonement you shall sound a horn all through your land.

Again the sound of the horn (*shofar*) signals a major event for the Israelites. The *shofar* is an animal horn hollowed out and always curved as opposed to some other horns that were straightened. The *shofar* is the one instrument that has survived in its ancient form to the present day. For these reasons, "ram's horn" is probably the best translation for this instrument.

The year of the jubilee was to be a year of release for people and property. After fifty years of accumulated debts, possibly even resulting in slavery, everyone was to return home to his own land and actually reclaim it. This must have been a great year of celebration. No wonder it was inaugurated with music.

Numbers

Instructions for Summoning People 10:1-10

2 "Make yourself two trumpets of silver, of hammered work you shall make them; and you shall use them for summoning the congregation and for having the camps set out.

3 "And when both are blown, all the congregation shall gather themselves to you at the doorway of the tent of meeting.

Numbers

4 "Yet if *only* one is blown, then the leaders, the heads of the divisions of Israel, shall assemble before you.
5 "But when you blow an alarm, the camps that are pitched on the east side shall set out.
6 "And when you blow an alarm the second time, the camps that are pitched on the south side shall set out; an alarm is to be blown for them to set out.
7 "When convening the assembly, however, you shall blow without sounding an alarm.
8 "The priestly sons of Aaron, moreover, shall blow the trumpets; and this shall be for you a perpetual statute throughout your generations.
9 "And when you go to war in your land against the adversary who attacks you, then you shall sound an alarm with the trumpets, that you may be remembered before the LORD your God, and be saved from your enemies.
10 "Also in the day of your gladness and in your appointed feasts, and on the first *days* of your months, you shall blow the trumpets over your burnt offerings, and over the sacrifices of your peace offerings; and they shall be as a reminder of you before your God. I am the LORD your God."

These detailed instructions again emphasize how important the trumpets were in communicating to this large group of people, possibly several million. I heard a speaker once lament the impersonal method of summoning a group of campers with a shrill whistle through the fingers. On the one hand I do understand his concern, but on the other hand, it is very effective for long distances and large groups of people. Somehow you need to get the attention of everyone. For Moses and the Levites the trumpets were extremely effective, I'm sure. In the subsequent accounts referring to the trumpet, it is frequently utilized to call the people together for a meeting.

This is also the first reference to the material to be used in the construction of these particular trumpets (*chatsotsrah*).

Numbers

They were to be made of silver. Whether they were earlier made of more natural materials such as the horns of animals we do not know. The trumpets or horns of those days did not have valves. This meant that they played only the natural harmonic scale, not the diatonic or chromatic scale as is possible on our present brass instruments.

Of course, this could be done on any tube with a mouthpiece on one end and a horn shape on the other. A garden hose with a funnel stuck in one end will serve as a trumpet; it might not sound all that great but it produces sound on the same principle. Also the Hebrew *taqa* indicates "to thrust, clap, give a blow, blast" as compared to the earlier *mashak* which suggested a drawing action.

Thanksgiving for Water 21:16-18
17 Then Israel sang this song:
"Spring up, O well! Sing to it!

There is no human physical need as acute as the need for water. The children of Israel had complained bitterly about their lack of food and water (and their loathing for the food they did have). This resulted in serpents and death and in salvation by looking at a bronze serpent fashioned by Moses. Irony of ironies —they were not to make graven images, and this one gave them life. Jesus, of course, referred to this as a sign pointing to His death on a cross that would bring salvation to all humanity. When the Israelites finally did get water, they burst forth into song like a gushing well that continues to bring refreshment to all.

Instruction for Assemblies 29:1-6
1 'Now in the seventh month, on the first day of the month, you shall also have a holy convocation; you shall do no laborious work. It will be to you a day for blowing trumpets.

Although trumpets are not actually indicated in the original, *teruah* (blowing) implies them.

Music in War 31:1-12
6 And Moses sent them, a thousand from each tribe, to the war, and Phinehas the son of Eleazar the priest, to the war with them, and the holy vessels and the trumpets for the alarm in his hand.

Before the nuclear age we couldn't imagine war without trumpets; now we can't imagine war with trumpets, except for ceremonial occasions. As we will see later, trumpets could be an integral part of the battle strategy to confuse or disorient the enemy. Then, the instruments and the sounds of soldiers would have been the only sounds you would hear on the battlefield. Now the sounds of guns, bombs, and aircraft would mask all of these, formerly natural, battle sounds.

Deuteronomy

The Lord Commands Moses to Compose 31:19-22, 30
19 "Now therefore, write this song for yourselves, and teach it to the sons of Israel; put it on their lips, in order that this song may be a witness for Me against the sons of Israel.

21 "Then it shall come about, when many evils and troubles have come upon them, that this song will testify before them as a witness (for it shall not be forgotten from the lips of their descendants); for I know their intent which they are developing today, before I have brought them into the land which I swore."

22 So Moses wrote this song the same day, and taught it to the sons of Israel.

30 Then Moses spoke in the hearing of all the assembly of Israel the words of this song, until they were complete:

Deuteronomy

This is what today is referred to as a swan song. Moses has completed his work and receives one final assignment from the Lord—to write a song of witness that implicates the Israelites when they stray from God. Not only did he compose it, he taught it to them. This is one of the last things Moses said, this and a blessing on the people that had caused him untold grief. We are often interested in the last words of well-known people. Here are some others:

Beethoven—"Plaudite, amici, comedia finita est"

Haydn—"God preserve the emperor!"

Mozart—"You spoke of refreshment, my Emilie. Take my last notes. Sit down to my piano here, and sing them to the hymn of your sainted mother. Let me hear once more those notes so long my solace and delight." When life was fleeting fast, the dying man called for his "Requiem," and musing said, "Did I not tell you that it was for myself that I composed this death-chant?"

So spoke some other great musicians on their death bed. The following song is, other than the blessing, Moses' "last words."

Moses' Last Composition 32:1-47

44 Then Moses came and spoke all the words of this song in the hearing of the people, he, with Joshua the son of Nun.

This hard-hitting song contains reminders of
    God's faithfulness
    Israel's infidelity
        Israel's foolishness
        God's wisdom
           God's care
           Israel's ingratitude
              Israel's corruption
              God's righteousness

along with similes, metaphors, hyperbole, personification, metonymy:

>grapes of poison
>honey from the rock
>consumed by plague
>carried on pinions of eagles
>the howling waste of the wilderness
>the high places of the earth
>
>vindication
>
>compassion

Joshua

The Fall of Jericho 6:1-21

4 "Also seven priests shall carry seven trumpets of rams' horns before the ark; then on the seventh day you shall march around the city seven times, and the priests shall blow the trumpets.

5 "And it shall be that when they make a long blast with the ram's horn, and when you hear the sound of the trumpet, all the people shall shout with a great shout; and the wall of the city will fall down flat, and the people will go up every man straight ahead."

6 So Joshua the son of Nun called the priests and said to them, "Take up the ark of the covenant, and let seven priests carry seven trumpets of rams' horns before the ark of the LORD."

8 And it was *so*, that when Joshua had spoken to the people, the seven priests carrying the seven trumpets of rams' horns before the LORD went forward and blew the trumpets; and the ark of the covenant of the LORD followed them.

9 And the armed men went before the priests who blew the trumpets, and the rear guard came after the ark, while they continued to blow the trumpets.

Joshua

13 And the seven priests carrying the seven trumpets of rams' horns before the ark of the LORD went on continually, and blew the trumpets; and the armed men went before them, and the rear guard came after the ark of the LORD, while they continued to blow the trumpets.

16 And it came about at the seventh time, when the priests blew the trumpets, Joshua said to the people, "Shout! For the LORD has given you the city."

20 So the people shouted, and *priests* blew the trumpets; and it came about, when the people heard the sound of the trumpet, that the people shouted with a great shout and the wall fell down flat, so that the people went up into the city, every man straight ahead, and they took the city.

The instructions for this battle were very detailed, but prefacing all of that is a very significant statement by God: "See, I have given Jericho into your hand, with its king *and* all the valiant warriors"(Josh. 6:2, italics in original). The victory was secured. All that was needed was for the people of God to follow instructions. This time they did.

This passage specifies both the *shofar* and the *yobel*, indicating two possibilities: the words were used interchangeably for the same instrument, or they were, in fact, two distinct instruments, both of which were played on this occasion. Since we are so frequently left with a lack of concrete information, a certain amount of speculation is always a factor. They are likely the "crooked trumpets" and not the straight silver trumpets used in the temple service. Then, to translate this as *ram's horn* is accurate.

It should also be noted that in war it was the ram's horn, with its undoubtedly shrill, piercing blast, that became the instrument of choice. With the strategy of using noise to confuse and overwhelm, utilizing this would certainly be an added benefit. One can imagine how unnerving it must have been for the people of

Joshua-Judges

Jericho to watch, and hear, the Israelites march around the city each day without attempting to take the city. This is a new battle strategy, and it was so because the Lord was in it.

Judges

Ehud Summoning Warriors 3:26-30
27 And it came about when he had arrived, that he blew the horn in the hill country of Ephraim; and the sons of Israel went down with him from the hill country, and he *was* in front of them.

The horn Ehud blew was the shofar.

Deborah and Barak's Song 5:1-31
1 Then Deborah and Barak the son of Abinoam sang on that day, saying,

> **2** "That the leaders led in Israel,
> That the people volunteered,
> Bless the LORD!
> **3** "Hear, O kings; give ear, O rulers!
> I—to the Lord, I will sing,
> I will sing praise to the LORD, the God of Israel.
>
> **10** "You who ride on white donkeys,
> You who sit on *rich* carpets,
> And you who travel on the road sing!
>
> **12** "Awake, awake, Deborah;
> Awake, awake, sing a song!
> Arise, Barak, and take away your captives, O son of Abinoam.
>
> **16** "Why did you sit among the sheepfolds,
> To hear the piping for the flocks?

Judges

Among the divisions of Reuben
There were great searchings of heart.

This, another lengthy song in the early history of the Israelites, has a similar context as the song of Moses after the crossing of the Red Sea. Both were sung after a major military victory. Moses sang with the men, Deborah and Barak apparently sang a duet. To recount what the Lord had done was their way of celebrating and giving honor to God as well as to the protagonists of the battle. In this case, as Deborah foretold, the honor went to a woman, Jael, the one who killed Sisera. Also, this account is clear in recognizing the leadership of Deborah in the conquest of the Caananites.

The composition is a mix of the sublime and the coarse, the reflective and the visceral, the past and the present, blessing and cursing, humility and pride, joy and sorrow. This expression of the extremes of emotion, sensory, and physical responses are common in the songs of the Old Testament, both those scattered throughout the historical and prophetic accounts as well as in the Psalms. Reading these expressions of praise to God makes one wonder why some of us as God's people are so reticent in attributing to God the events in our life and in our country. Most of our contemporary Christian songs sound very bland when juxtaposed against a song like this.

Gideon Summoning Warriors 6:33-35

34 So the Spirit of the Lord came upon Gideon; and he blew a trumpet, and the Abiezerites were called together to follow him.

Gideon Defeats the Midianites 7:1-25

8 So the 300 men took the people's provisions and their trumpets into their hands. And Gideon sent all the *other* men of Israel, each to his tent, but retained the 300 men; and the camp of Midian was below him in the valley.

Judges

16 And he divided the 300 men into three companies, and he put trumpets and empty pitchers into the hands of all of them, with torches inside the pitchers.

18 "When I and all who are with me blow the trumpet, then you also blow the trumpets all around the camp, and say, 'For the LORD and for Gideon.'"

19 So Gideon and the hundred men who were with him came to the outskirts of the camp at the beginning of the middle watch, when they had just posted the watch; and they blew the trumpets and smashed the pitchers that were in their hands.

20 When the three companies blew the trumpets and broke the pitchers, they held the torches in their left hands and the trumpets in their right hands for blowing, and cried, "A sword for the LORD and for Gideon!"

22 And when they blew 300 trumpets, the LORD set the sword of one against another even throughout the whole army; and the army fled as far as Beth-shittah toward Zererah, as far as the edge of Abel-meholah, by Tabbath.

When Gideon was directed by God to select the, so to speak, elite corps for the battle against the Midianites, God indicated several criteria, some of which had little to do with prowess on the battlefield. The first was fearlessness, certainly a desirable quality for a soldier; the second was lapping water from the hands rather than kneeling at the water, possibly indicating more watchfulness; the third, (seldom, if ever, noted) was that they all had to be able to play the trumpet. The passage reiterates the fact that there were three hundred men all of whom were issued trumpets and all of whom blew them at the appointed time. This might seem insignificant to those who have never attempted to produce a sound on a brass instrument, but to those who are aware of the difficulties, this can be seen as quite remarkable. In any case, the combination of the breaking of the

Judges

pitchers with resultant bright light from the torches till then hidden, the loud shout, "A sword for the LORD and for Gideon," and the blast of three hundred trumpets totally disoriented and diffused the Midianite army throughout the countryside. The disconcerting effects of the music of the trumpet are seen again and again in the battle scenes of the Old Testament. The tradition of combining the music of brass instruments with the military is certainly an old one.

Jephthah's Daughter 11:29-40

34 When Jephthah came to his house at Mizpah, behold, his daughter was coming out to meet him with tambourines and with dancing. Now she was his one *and* only child; besides her he had neither son nor daughter.

The fact that the Hebrew word *toph* is here translated *tambourine* and in the Exodus 15 account is translated *timbrel* is interesting, but becomes somewhat trivial in the context of the pathos of the narrative. The rash, and we would say unwise, vow of a father condemns his only daughter to, at the very least, a life of virginity in a culture where one of the highest honors was to bear children. By making and carrying out this vow, Jephthah effectively terminated his family line. The passage in verse 31 indicates that Jephthah's vow allowed for two possibilities for the daughter. One was that she was to be dedicated to the Lord for a life of virginity and the other that she was to be burnt as an offering to the Lord. The former seems to be the how the vow was honored, when it is indicated in verse 39 that she never had relations with any man.

Wives for the Benjamites 21:19-24

21 and watch; and behold, if the daughters of Shiloh come out to take part in the dances, then you shall come out of the vineyards and each of you shall catch his wife from the daughters of Shiloh, and go to the land of Benjamin.

Judges-1 Samuel

23 And the sons of Benjamin did so, and took wives according to their number from those who danced, whom they carried away. And they went and returned to their inheritance, and rebuilt the cities and lived in them.

The artistic expressions of the day obviously often occurred in the outdoors. The dancing and the music, especially in war, were outside. The natural was combined with the natural. This is definitely different today where most cultural, artistic events, especially in the Northern Hemisphere, are designed to occur in the enclosed, sanitized, carefully designed structures known as concert halls. The artistic expression can be more controlled, more refined, but on the other hand also loses some of its familiarity, intimacy, and spontaneity.

Ruth

There are no references to music in the Book of Ruth.

First Samuel

Saul Prophesying 10:1-13
5 "Afterward you will come to the hill of God where the Philistine garrison is; and it shall be as soon as you have come there to the city, that you will meet a group of prophets coming down from the high place with harp, tambourine, flute, and a lyre before them, and they will be prophesying.

The significant concept in this passage relates to the integration of music and prophesy. These prophets, presumably from a training school for young prophets, were prophesying (teaching) in the context of music. Musicians in the church today often do not recognize their ministry as a teaching ministry and as a

1 Samuel

result, in the contemporary social milieu are therefore often seen by others as simply Christian entertainers.

Although this event is often cited as an example of the folk music of the prophets as compared to the liturgical music of the Levitical ministry, the connection between music and the ministry of the Word is immediately obvious. As the musician is often consumed in the development of music skills, so he must also be immersed in the study of the Word to forge a combination that has a potential for a potent ministry to the people of God.

One of the instruments mentioned here is the harp, sometimes translated as *psaltery* and in the original, *nebel,* possibly a ten-stringed instrument as indicated in Psalm 33:2 and in Psalm 144:9. A second, the tambourine, or a tabret or timbrel *(toph),* has been discussed earlier. The flute *(chalil)* is obviously a wind instrument with its root meaning being "to bore or pierce." The final one is the *kinnor,* a harp or possibly lyre.

Jonathan Smites the Philistines 13:1-4

3 And Jonathan smote the garrison of the Philistines that was in Geba, and the Philistines heard of *it.* Then Saul blew the trumpet throughout the land, saying, "Let the Hebrews hear."

Saul Engages David as Court Musician 16:14-23

16 "Let our lord now command your servants who are before you. Let them seek a man who is a skillful player on the harp; and it shall come about when the evil spirit from God is on you, that he shall play *the harp* with his hand, and you will be well."

17 So Saul said to his servants, "Provide for me now a man who can play well, and bring *him* to me."

18 Then one of the young men answered and said, "Behold, I have seen a son of Jesse the Bethlehemite who is a skillful musician, a mighty man of valor, a warrior, one prudent in

1 Samuel

speech, and a handsome man; and the LORD is with him."

23 So it came about whenever the *evil* spirit from God came to Saul, David would take the harp and play *it* with his hand; and Saul would be refreshed and be well, and the evil spirit would depart from him.

This musician was much more than skillful on the harp, as we later discover once he is king. He is described by his acquaintance as a skillful musician, a mighty man of valor, a warrior, one prudent in speech, a handsome man, and a companion of the Lord. On an earlier occasion (verse 12), when Samuel was searching for a new king, he was described as ruddy, with beautiful eyes and a handsome appearance. In addition, when he was anointed by Samuel, the Spirit of the Lord came mightily upon David. This was quite a musician, quite a man. Can you imagine the riots he would have caused if he had been a contemporary, popular musician?

But from a musical standpoint what is interesting here is that music was seen to be the antidote to the attacks on King Saul by an evil spirit (and from God no less). The therapeutic effects of music, for centuries known by musicians and others alike, has in this century been studied and confirmed by many researchers and applied in situations of mental illness, mental handicap, old age, and emotional instability with very positive results.

Although the music had a healing, soothing effect on Saul, the musical medicine did not heal the hate that developed in the heart of Saul. After the slaying of Goliath, Saul tried on two occasions to kill David while he was playing the harp for Saul. This confirms our intuitive ideas that music never has an absolute uncontrollable power over anyone. The arguments sometimes given about certain types of music that are purported to have certain inevitable effects cannot be proven. Sinful acts are decisions and cannot be blamed on circumstances around us that in

1 Samuel

any case we could also often control if we decided to do so. Saul was finally overcome by the hate that he allowed to grow within him.

Women Praise David 18:6-9

6 And it happened as they were coming, when David returned from killing the Philistine, that the women came out of all the cities of Israel, singing and dancing, to meet King Saul, with tambourines, with joy and with musical instruments.

7 And the women sang as they played, and said,

> "Saul has slain his thousands,
> And David his ten thousands."

For David this adulation was deadly. Until now Saul had seen David as a young, harmless musician. But little did Saul know this seemingly innocent youth was not only much more than a cherubic harpist, but already anointed by Samuel to be the next king. The question he asks, "Now what more can he have but the kingdom?" is ironically prophetic. Saul's anger turns to suspicion and then to murder, which he, however, is never able to carry out.

Saul Tries to Kill David 18:10-11

10 Now it came about on the next day that an evil spirit from God came mightily upon Saul, and he raved in the midst of the house, while David was playing *the harp* with his hand, as usual; and a spear *was* in Saul's hand.

By now Saul is maddened with the frustration of knowing that the Lord has left him and that the kingdom is slipping away from him. The music, which once provided relief from the evil spirit, now is an irritant and catalyst to evil actions.

Saul Tries to Kill David Again 19:9-10

9 Now there was an evil spirit from the LORD on Saul as he was sitting in his house with his spear in his hand, and David was playing *the harp* with *his* hand.

Saul tries to kill again.

David Feigns Madness 21:10-15

11 But the servants of Achish said to him, "Is this not David the king of the land? Did they not sing of this one as they danced, saying,

> 'Saul has slain his thousands,
> And David his ten thousands'?"

David's reputation is secure and widespread, and in this case he is not willing to be recognized as the man who was the subject of the women's song at one time. The only way to save his life was to feign insanity. It worked.

David, Achish, and the Philistines 29:1-5

5 "Is this not David, of whom they sing in the dances, saying,

> 'Saul has slain his thousands,
> And David his ten thousands'?"

It is somewhat remarkable that David, who some time before had killed the Philistines' hero Goliath, was here spared by Achish, a Philistine.

David Rescues His Wives and Goods 30:16-20

16 And when he had brought him down, behold, they were spread over all the land, eating and drinking and dancing because of all the great spoil that they had taken from the land of the Philistines and from the land of Judah.

Dancing *(chagag)* continued to be a response to victory. In this case it was the Amalekites who danced after capturing David's family and property. Here, however, the word used to describe their activity is not the usual *mecholah* but *chagag* which means "to make a pilgrimage, keep a pilgrim feast."

Second Samuel

David Sorrows for Jonathan 1:17-27
17 Then David chanted with this lament over Saul and Jonathan his son,
18 and he told *them* to teach the sons of Judah *the song* of the bow; behold, it is written in the book of Jashar.

King David also chants (*qonen*) for Abner (2 Samuel 3:33) when he is killed. The other two occasions when this Hebrew term is used are in 2 Chronicles 35:25 and Ezekiel 32:16.

How do music and sorrow intersect? For David, whose life was intertwined with music, the expression of one of his most sorrowful times was best articulated through music, in this situation, a chanted lament. But must there be music? Funerals usually do have music. We sing but we don't really feel like singing. Must we sing? The Scriptures have a few accounts of singing at sad events, but by far the majority of occasions for music are joyful events. Although music can express grief, it is not as natural a vehicle for sorrow as for gladness. In my opinion it is proper not to have music when we are grieving and it is proper to have it. To some, music is a great comfort when someone has passed away, and the healing of the soul is accomplished by listening to music. But don't force it on one who does not respond in that way (see also Isaiah 24:7-23, Job 30:24-31, Psalm 30:10-12, and Lamentations 5:1-18).

The subject matter of this song, the one David chanted and commanded that it be sung by the sons of Judah, shows the character of a remarkable man. Although he deeply mourned the death of Jonathan his bosom friend, the song speaks as often of Saul the king who hunted him like an animal to kill and

2 Samuel

destroy him. Not only does he recall Saul, he recalls positive memories and urges the people to mourn for Saul, the king who had, by the time he died, lost all contact with God and lost all respect of the people of Israel. Here in this song is some evidence of why God called David a man after His own heart. He was truly a man without guile.

Joab Pursues Abner 2:24-29

28 So Joab blew the trumpet; and all the people halted and pursued Israel no longer, nor did they continue to fight anymore.

Joab calls a truce on the trumpet *(shofar)* and lets Abner escape, but as we shall see later, the reprieve for Abner is only temporary.

David Sorrows for Abner 3:31-39

31 Then David said to Joab and to all the people who were with him, "Tear your clothes and gird on sackcloth and lament before Abner." And King David walked behind the bier.

33 And the king chanted a *lament* for Abner and said,
"Should Abner die as a fool dies?

Victory Celebration by David 6:1-23

5 Meanwhile, David and all the house of Israel were celebrating before the LORD with all kinds of *instruments made of* fir wood, and with lyres, harps, tambourines, castanets and cymbals.

14 And David was dancing before the LORD with all *his* might, and David was wearing a linen ephod.

15 So David and all the house of Israel were bringing up the ark of the LORD with shouting and the sound of the trumpet.

16 Then it happened *as* the ark of the LORD came into the city of David that Michal the daughter of Saul looked out of the window and saw King David leaping and dancing before the LORD; and she despised him in her heart.

2 Samuel

David has just been anointed for the third time: the first time by Samuel as the one chosen by God to lead the country after King Saul, the second time by the people of Judah, and now finally by the Israelites. It is after the first victory against the Philistines by the united country that the people celebrate with all these instruments. Two new instruments are mentioned here: the *menaanea*, possibly a percussion instrument that was struck or shaken, here translated *castanets*, and the *tseltselim*, which means to tingle or tinkle, here translated *cymbals*. The major reason for the celebration was that the ark had been recovered and was to be moved back to its proper location.

The interruption to the event is the troubling incident of the death of Uzzah for attempting to steady the ark because the oxen nearly upset it. A prior error was made in that they were carrying the ark on a cart pulled by oxen when men should have been carrying it. God, it seems finally, punished them when Uzzah touched the ark.

The subject of dancing has been a matter of contention among Evangelical Christians for a long time, although it seems that in some circles there has been an acceptance that has gradually come upon us without a great struggle. In our society there are several different types of dancing: (1) dancing for entertainment, which includes formal ballroom dancing and the more spontaneous dance at events such as rock concerts; (2) folk dancing, which varies greatly with different cultures and is often very rigorous and intricate, requiring great energy and skill; and (3) liturgical dance that is intended to lead and involve believers in their worship. Another simple way of differentiating dance would be to label them as formal or spontaneous.

Vigorous physical activity seems to be the type of dancing that David did here as he led the victory parade to return the ark to its home. For David this was a victory dance that credited God

2 Samuel

with the defeat of the Philistines. Although the account indicates that he was dancing before the Lord and presumably had no intention of drawing attention to himself, he certainly drew the ire of his wife Michal, whose attitude brought upon her the curse of childlessness. The writer emphasizes that David was dancing before the Lord, an attitude that is of utmost importance if we as believers seek in some way to defend dancing as a Christian act of worship.

The linen ephod is also of significance in that it was priestly garb, not royal or military apparel. Here is the warrior king who has conquered, and instead of leading the parade as a king, he leads it as a priest leading his people in a praise parade to honor God. It is an attempt to direct the glory to Jehovah, and with that divert the attention from himself. Whether he was successful is debatable.

Absalom's Treason 15:1-12
10 But Absalom sent spies throughout all the tribes of Israel, saying, "As soon as you hear the sound of the trumpet, then you shall say, 'Absalom is king in Hebron.'"

As with any other good thing, trumpets or other instruments can be used to do evil. Here the trumpet, which has been used to signal for events calling people to obedience to God, is used to incite to evil, rebellion against the king God anointed.

Absalom Killed 18:9-18
16 Then Joab blew the trumpet, and the people returned from pursuing Israel, for Joab restrained the people.

David and Barzillai 19:31-39
35 "I am now eighty years old. Can I distinguish between good and bad? Or can your servant taste what I eat or what I drink? Or can I hear anymore the voice of singing men and women? Why then should your servant be an added burden to my lord the king?

2 Samuel

This passage indicates to some extent the effects of age on the perception of music. Barzillai realizes that his enjoyment of music is far from what it was when he was a younger man. Studies have shown that physically we begin to deteriorate at about age twenty, and that includes our hearing. This might occur sooner if our ears are abused by high decibels of sound. By the time old age comes on us, many of the higher and lower extremes of frequencies are gone, and with it the richness of timbre and pitch that we enjoy when we're young. If you enjoy music, take care of your ears.

Sheba's Treason 20:1-22

1 Now a worthless fellow happened to be there whose name was Sheba, the son of Bichri, a Benjamite; and he blew the trumpet and said, "We have no portion in David, Nor do we have inheritance in the son of Jesse; Every man to his tents, O Israel!"

22 Then the woman wisely came to all the people. And they cut off the head of Sheba the son of Bichri and threw it to Joab. So he blew the trumpet, and they were dispersed from the city, each to his tent. Joab also returned to the king at Jerusalem.

The *shofar* really could be called the war trumpet because it is invariably in use in times of battle, whether it's by Sheba, a rebel giving the signal, or Joab, the faithful general of King David.

David's Victory Song 22:1-51

1 And David spoke the words of this song to the LORD in the day that the LORD delivered him from the hand of all his enemies and from the hand of Saul.

50 "Therefore I will give thanks to Thee,
O LORD, among the nations,
And I will sing praises to Thy name.

The song given here is almost identical to Psalm 18. The

2 Samuel-1 Kings

English variations seem to be translation variations rather than meaning variations. The life context for David is certainly a significant one because he spent so much of his life fleeing from his enemies, although the ones that hurt him most were those very closely associated with him, King Saul and Absalom.

The psalm is consumed with thoughts of the greatness of God and the mighty works He had performed in protecting David. All that David had done receives little attention. The thesis statement, "The LORD is my rock and my fortress and my deliverer," is developed in a barrage of poetic images that leave no doubt as to David's perception, or rather conviction, about who was responsible for all these acts.

David's Last Song 23:1-7

1 Now these are the last words of David. David the son of Jesse declares, And the man who was raised on high declares, The anointed of the God of Jacob, And the sweet psalmist of Israel,

The last words of David are, predictably, poetry. Throughout his life, David responded to the circumstances in his life, whether adverse or favorable, by writing Psalms that were then sung by others to express their own responses to similar events.

First Kings

Solomon's Coronation 1:32-48

34 "And let Zadok the priest and Nathan the prophet anoint him there as king over Israel, and blow the trumpet and say, '*Long* live King Solomon!'

39 Zadok the priest then took the horn of oil from the tent and anointed Solomon. Then they blew the trumpet, and all the people said, '*Long* live King Solomon!'

40 And all the people went up after him, and the people

1 Kings

were playing on flutes and rejoicing with great joy, so that the earth shook at their noise.

41 Now Adonijah and all the guests who were with him heard *it*, as they finished eating. When Joab heard the sound of the trumpet, he said, "Why is the city making such an uproar?"

This celebration is a familiar one, even in our day. When a monarch is crowned there is great celebration with all the pomp that the country can muster. In Israel there had been coups and rebellions (again also a contemporary scene for us), mostly originating from King David's sons. Finally the heir of, presumably, David's choosing is crowned and the nation of Israel is launched into a long period of relative peace.

The celebration is a loud one. We think that with our technology we have been able to produce decibels of sound beyond what could have been imagined by the people of biblical times, but I'm not so sure. This account indicates that from the trumpet, the people, and the flutes "the earth shook at their noise" (v. 40). Joab, hearing the noise, asks, "Why is the city making such an uproar?" This was one noisy celebration. Other accounts in the Old Testament suggest extremely loud musical occasions that should cause us to be cautious criticizing an event that is loud simply because it's loud. The Scriptures do not really say that music should be loud, neither do they say that it should be soft. I do, however, realize that when the ears start bleeding and permanent hearing loss occurs because of high volume, there is cause for concern, just as in industry when there is excessive noise.

Solomon's Wisdom 4:29-34

31 For he was wiser than all men, than Ethan the Ezrahite, Heman, Calcol and Darda, the sons of Mahol; and his fame was known in all the surrounding nations.

32 He also spoke 3,000 proverbs, and his songs were 1,005.

1 Kings-2 Kings

These 1,005 songs have apparently been lost except for the few preserved in the Psalms. Without a doubt, Solomon was a very gifted king and did much more than administer his kingdom.

Instruments of Almug Trees 10:11,12
12 And the king made of the almug trees supports for the house of the LORD and for the king's house, also lyres and harps for the singers; such almug trees have not come in *again*, nor have they been seen to this day.

The almug tree was apparently useful for several types of building: larger structures such as temples and palaces as well as the more intricate musical instruments. The almug tree, according to this passage, became extinct, at least in this area, possibly because of the heavy demand for it.

A further musical point that needs noting is that the lyres and harps were built for the singers, indicating that they were likely used as accompanying instruments and not only as solo or orchestral instruments.

Second Kings

Elisha Prophesies 3:13-20
15 "But now bring me a minstrel." And it came about, when the minstrel played, that the hand of the LORD came upon him.

This is a most fascinating story. The kings of Israel, Judah, and Edom have joined forces to go against the Moabites and, in their maneuvers, find themselves in a situation where there is no water for the army and the cattle. It is a definite case of inadequate scouting and planning. It seems a considerable leap from Elisha having poured water over Elijah's hands to supplying water for this huge horde of men and animals, but to them it seems a reasonable expectation. After all, when a king, not one

2 Kings

but three, commands, there must be an immediate execution of the request. And Elisha is able to gratify.

But the process, for a musician, is particularly interesting. When Elisha needs wisdom from the Lord he requests a minstrel (he presumably was not skillful or trained in music as many prophets were) and seeks the Lord's word as the music is played. The music was a catalyst that brought inspiration to Elisha. Then he gave instructions to the kings that brought them not only water but later also victory. As the minstrel played the hand of the Lord came upon Elisha and he was able to provide the immediate physical needs of the army as well as military advice.

A musician must be willing to provide the ambience or milieu to make that word from the Lord easier to discern. Is music always necessary? Can it be distracting rather than helpful? Would silence more often be the better alternative? There needs to be sensitivity to the needs and inclinations of individuals. Speaking personally, I have to say that even though I'm a musician, or maybe because I'm one, I find music distracting when someone is praying or speaking; I tend to listen to the music rather than to the other activity, whatever that might be. On this occasion it was the prophet who needed music to help him in his contemplation. As musicians we need to be willing to provide that ministry when it is needed. However, I am not entirely convinced that we do a service to the average congregation when we make them listen to several messages simultaneously even though one of them is music.

Jehu Anointed 9:11-13

13 Then they hurried and each man took his garment and placed it under him on the bare steps, and blew the trumpet, saying, "Jehu is king!"

2 Kings-1 Chronicles

Athaliah Killed 11:13-16
14 And she looked and behold, the king was standing by the pillar, according to the custom, with the captains and the trumpeters beside the king; and all the people of the land rejoiced and blew trumpets. Then Athaliah tore her clothes and cried, "Treason! Treason!"

Collection for Temple Repair 12:9-16
13 But there were not made for the house of the LORD silver cups, snuffers, bowls, trumpets, any vessels of gold, or vessels of silver from the money which was brought into the house of the LORD;

The repair work of the temple here undertaken was the work of King Jehoash, of whom it is said in verse 2 of chapter 12 that he "did right in the sight of the LORD all his days in which Jehoiada the priest instructed him." This was a king, different from many of the others, who was willing to take instruction and lived a consistent, godly life pleasing to the Lord. There will be times when leaders are willing to be mentored. When that happens, there is the potential for great leadership and great following.

As a part of his service to the Lord Jehoash repaired the temple but in this case that did not include the smaller implements listed in the above passage. Trumpets *(chatsotsrah)* are listed with a variety of vessels and other items used in the Levites' ministries in the temple rituals. The musical instruments were obviously an integral part of the necessary items for the temple activities.

First Chronicles

Levite Musicians 6:31-48
31 Now these are those whom David appointed over the

1 Chronicles

service of song in the house of the LORD, after the ark rested *there.*

32 And they ministered with song before the tabernacle of the tent of meeting, until Solomon had built the house of the LORD in Jerusalem; and they served in their office according to their order.

33 And these are those who served with their sons. From the sons of the Kohathites *were* Heman the singer, the son of Joel, the son of Samuel,

39 And *Heman's* brother Asaph stood at his right hand, even Asaph the son of Berechiah, the son of Shimea,

44 And on the left hand *were* their kinsmen the sons of Merari: Ethan the son of Kishi, the son of Abdi, the son of Malluch,

It is only when we get to Chronicles that we are finally told about the Levites' musical duties. Not only that, specific personnel who were appointed to these ministries are named in a genealogical list that connects each one to Levi, whose tribe was responsible for all the temple ministrations. This passage, in particular, lists those who ministered in song with their sons. These three men who were Levites, and possibly related, are each traced back to specific larger Levite families: Heman to Kohath, Asaph to Gershon, and Ethan to Merari. Each of these musicians contributed at least one poem to the Book of Psalms, with Asaph providing at least Psalms 73 to 83. In this dynasty of singers it seems that Korah, a son of Kohath, had sons who were particularly gifted in singing because many of the Psalms are written for the sons of Korah.

Levite Musicians 9:33-34

33 Now these are the singers, heads of fathers' *households* of the Levites, *who lived* in the chambers *of the temple*

1 Chronicles

free *from other service;* for they were engaged in their work day and night.

This passage indicates the extent to which the Levites were expected to serve in the affairs of the temple. They were, what we would today call, full-time Christian workers who devoted all their time to the temple service. God, in His instructions, was very explicit about the financial support structure of the Levite tribe. They were all to be involved in the ministry and did not have any land allotted to them on which they could support their families; all of that was to come from the other tribes. To extrapolate from this to today is somewhat difficult, but it is instructive. It appears that we could enlarge our vision a bit as to who could or should be set free to minister to the rest of us in a full-time capacity.

One might ask what proportion of the Israelites were Levites. In the numbering of the nation we are given the number of men for each tribe, and this could indicate at least how many there were when the people left Egypt.

Reuben	43,730
Simeon	22,200
Gad	45,500
Judah	76,500
Issachar	64,300
Zebulun	60,500
Manasseh	52,700
Ephraim	32,500
Benjamin	45,600
Dan	64,400
Asher	53,400
Napthtali	45,400
Levi	23,000
TOTAL	629,730

1 Chronicles

The calculation to determine the proportion of Levites to the rest of the Israelites indicates that about 3.5 percent of the nation were Levites. We could therefore say that a congregation should consider supporting at least this proportion in some full-time ministry, some of whom would be musicians. Now in all of this we need to remember that we have considered only the men, because they were the only ones counted in this census. If women and children were included in the calculation, and they should be, the numbers would obviously change somewhat.

David Moves the Ark 13:1-14
8 And David and all Israel were celebrating before God with all *their* might, even with songs and with lyres, harps, tambourines, cymbals, and with trumpets.

The musical terms in this passage are as follows: songs *(shir)*, lyres *(kinnor)*, harps *(nebel)*, tambourines *(toph)*, cymbals *(metsiltayim)*, and trumpets *(chatsotrah)*. This passage is parallel to 2 Samuel 6. In both accounts we are told of King David's leadership in the celebration of the return of the ark of God. David had consulted with all the leaders and received strong affirmation to bring the ark back to Jerusalem. This plan, however, was aborted by the death of Uzza, who, out of concern for the ark, reached out to steady it.

There were several things that might have contributed to the Lord's judgment here. One was that the Levites had been carefully instructed on how to carry and care for the ark. It was never to be on a cart; it was to be carried. Also, we do not know whether Uzza was, in fact, a Levite. We might argue that God was less severe with the Philistines, but they also understood very quickly that to possess the ark was not a benefit to them, as it had been for the Israelites. The Israelites had been instructed regarding the ark but were not obeying, possibly because the king was not sufficiently familiar or concerned about the procedures.

The ark had, about twenty years earlier, been seized by the

1 Chronicles

Philistines (1 Samuel 5) who thought that since the ark was a "good luck charm" for the Israelites, it would be the same for them. This thoroughly backfired, and in a short time they were begging the Israelites to take the ark back, which they did. On the one hand, the ark was a blessing to the Israelites, but was a curse to the Philistines. It was a curse to Uzza, but was a blessing to Obed-edom the Gittite.

Apart from these details, there is the verse that describes David's celebration of the return of the ark. "David and all Israel were celebrating before God with all *their* might." David was able to rally all the people: what a sight it must have been! This was not one of the liturgical events that would have been carefully orchestrated by the Levites, but was a spontaneous event motivated by the return of an icon and a king who recognized the significance of this for the people.

Levite Musicians 15:16-29

16 Then David spoke to the chiefs of the Levites to appoint their relatives the singers, with instruments of music, harps, lyres, loud-sounding cymbals, to raise sounds of joy.

19 So the singers, Heman, Asaph, and Ethan w*ere appointed* to sound aloud cymbals of bronze;
20 and Zechariah, Aziel, Shemiramoth, Jehiel, Unni, Eliab, Maaseiah, and Benaiah, with harps *tuned* to alamoth;
21 and Mattithiah, Eliphelehu, Mikneiah, Obed-edom, Jeiel, and Azaziah, to lead with lyres tuned to the sheminith.
22 And Chenaniah, chief of the Levites, was *in charge of* the singing; he gave instruction in singing because he was skillful.

24 And Shebaniah, Joshaphat, Nethanel, Amasai, Zechariah, Benaiah, and Eliezer, the priests, blew the trumpets before the ark of God. Obed-edom and Jehiah also *were* gatekeepers for the ark.

27 Now David was clothed with a robe of fine linen with all the Levites who were carrying the ark, and the singers and

1 Chronicles

Chenaniah the leader of the singing *with* the singers. David also wore an ephod of linen.

28 Thus all Israel brought up the ark of the covenant of the LORD with shouting, and with sound of the horn, with trumpets, with loud-sounding cymbals, with harps and lyres.

Finally, the ark of the covenant is brought back to Jerusalem, and this time the Levites are definitely in the procession in all of their celebrity splendor. It should be noted that the ark is being carried by the Levites, as it should be.

Musically there are two significant points: the musicians named and the musical resources utilized. Three Levites again are listed as the prominent leaders: Heman, Asaph, and Ethan. These were the lead singers and generally the leaders in this celebration event. Many others who had specific responsibilities are also listed.

Second, the passage indicates the instruments that were in use for this parade. The two events, the movement of the ark from the Philistines to Obed-edom and the movement from Obed-edom to Jerusalem are both recorded in Chronicles and Samuel. A comparison of the original words and translations for the instruments used in the parade are as follows:

2 Samuel 6:1-11
to Obed-edom

Hebrew	NASB
	instruments made (implied) of fir wood
	lyres *(kinnor)*
	harps *(nebel)*
	tambourines *(toph)*
	castanets *(menaanea)*
	cymbals *(tseltselim)*

1 Chronicles

2 Samuel 6:12-23
to Jerusalem
Hebrew   NASB
               trumpet *(shophar)*

1 Chronicles 13:1-14
to Obed-edom
Hebrew   NASB
               songs *(shir)*
               lyres *(kinnor)*
               harps *(nebel)*
               tambourines *(toph)*
               cymbals *(metsiltayim)*
               trumpets *(chatsotsrah)*

1 Chronicles 15:16-29
to Jerusalem
Hebrew   NASB
               instruments *(keli)*
               singers *(shir)*
               horn *(shophar)*
               trumpets *(chatsotsrah)*
               loud-sounding
               cymbals *(shamametsiltayim)*
               harps *(nebel)*
               lyres *(kinnor)*

One new term needs some comment. *Keli,* translated instruments in this and other passages, literally means *utensil* or *vessel.* In Nigeria and other African countries, jugs made of clay are still used as percussive musical instruments. They are made in several different sizes and styles to provide a solid thumping sound that that has a very unique timbre when combined with several other indigenous percussion instruments. Utilizing common domestic items was apparently common in the Middle East

1 Chronicles

and certainly is still a widespread practice in Nigeria and other African countries.

Levite Musicians and Their Song 16:1-43

4 And he appointed some of the Levites *as* ministers before the ark of the LORD, even to celebrate and to thank and praise the LORD God of Israel:

5 Asaph the chief, and second to him Zechariah, *then* Jeiel, Shemiramoth, Jehiel, Mattithiah, Eliab, Benaiah, Obed-edom, and Jeiel, with musical instruments, harps, lyres; also Asaph played loud-sounding cymbals,

6 and Benaiah and Jahaziel the priests *blew* trumpets continually before the ark of the covenant of God.

9 Sing to Him, sing praises to Him; Speak of all His wonders.

> **33** Then the trees of the forest will sing for joy before the LORD; For He is coming to judge the earth.

42 And with them *were* Heman and Jeduthun *with* trumpets and cymbals for those who should sound aloud, and *with* instruments *for* the songs of God, and the sons of Jeduthun for the gate.

These passages in Chronicles continue to emphasize the role of the Levites in the music ministry. An elaborate network of Levite musical leaders and their assistants keep recurring in the record of musical activities related to the ministry in the tabernacle. These ministers were to celebrate and to thank and praise the Lord before the ark of the covenant. Particularly on this day, when the ark had been returned, they were instructed to sing and the psalm they sang is recorded for us in verses 8 to 36. At the end of this passage David instructs the Levites he has appointed to continually offer burnt offerings to the Lord and give thanks to the Lord because his lovingkindness is everlasting.

1 Chronicles

This giving of thanks was to be led by Heman and Jeduthun with instruments that produced loud sounds. These instruments included the domestic vessels designated as *keli,* as discussed in the previous passage. They were to accompany the songs of God. The argument that loud music is not pleasing to God will need to have a different basis than the Scriptures because too often the music of the Levites is described as loud. This, of course, is relative to some level of sound that we can't determine at this point, but in relation to what they had then it was loud.

Levite Musicians 23:1-6
5 and 4,000 *were* gatekeepers, and 4,000 *were* praising the LORD with the instruments which David made for giving praise.

Earlier in the passage we are told that the census indicated that there were 38,000 Levites over thirty years of age at the time when King David reached old age and handed the kingdom over to his son Solomon. Of these, 4,000 were to praise the Lord with instruments (again *keli)* made by David. That is an impressive proportion of the Levites who were to be involved in the music ministry.

In fact, the Levites work was assigned as follows:
> 24,000 overseers of the work of the house of the Lord
> 6,000 officers and judges
> 4,000 gatekeepers
> 4,000 praising the Lord with the instruments of David

Levite Musicians 25:1-31
1 Moreover, David and the commanders of the army set apart for the service *some* of the sons of Asaph and of Heman and of Jeduthun, who *were* to prophesy with lyres, harps, and cymbals; and the number of those who performed their service was:

1 Chronicles

2 Of the sons of Asaph: Zaccur, Joseph, Nethaniah, and Asharelah; the sons of Asaph *were* under the direction of Asaph, who prophesied under the direction of the king.
3 Of Jeduthun, the sons of Jeduthun: Gedaliah, Zeri, Jeshaiah, Shimei, Hashabiah, and Mattithiah, six, under the direction of their father Jeduthun with the harp, who prophesied in giving thanks and praising the LORD.
4 Of Heman, the sons of Heman: Bukkiah, Mattaniah, Uzziel, Shebuel and Jerimoth, Hananiah, Hanani, Eliathah, Giddalti and Romamti-ezer, Joshbekashah, Mallothi, Hothir, Mahazioth.
5 All these *were* the sons of Heman the king's seer to exalt him according to the words of God, for God gave fourteen sons and three daughters to Heman.
6 All these *were* under the direction of their father to sing in the house of the LORD, with cymbals, harps and lyres, for the service of the house of God. Asaph, Jeduthun and Heman *were* under the direction of the king.
7 And their number who were trained in singing to the LORD, with their relatives, all who were skillful, *was* 288.

"Honor to whom honor is due" seems to be the attitude as name after name is listed, and in this case the names of the musicians. Whereas in an earlier passage in chapter 6, the writer traces the genealogical lines of the trio Asaph, Heman, and Ethan back to Levi, here the sons of the trio, Asaph, Heman, and Jeduthun are listed. These men were not only musicians, they were prophets who prophesied in their ministry of music. They were to exalt the Lord according to the words of God. This places a heavy responsibility on the musician who purports to speak a message from the Lord.

Too many take this too lightly and are in fact speaking their own message, one that entertains and makes a living but does not provide the message that the people of God, and the world, need. It is particularly incumbent on Christian musicians today,

1 Chronicles-2 Chronicles

who are often able to make a living (and quite a fine one at that), to search their hearts to determine why they are doing the music they are doing.

The accountability is less reliable when it is the market rather than the church that determines what the composer will produce. If those musicians who seriously want to minister would be willing to give all their income to the church and then live on a salary, I suspect the Christian music scene would change dramatically. That is one of the reasons why the ministry of Billy Graham has had such longevity compared to some others who have had a similar focus in their work.

There is a further emphasis that needs noting here. These 288 singers were trained and skillful in their craft. Although the temple musicians were all chosen from the Levitical tribe, they were not automatically in a choir or orchestra. The individuals who were chosen were trained to the point where they were then considered skillful in their field of musical endeavor. We should expect no less in our church ministries. Too often the young, aspiring musician tries to short-circuit the tedium of training and seeks to get to the top of a perceived pinnacle by plying a craft before the dues of hard work have been paid. The musicians of the Bible were not able to do this.

Second Chronicles

Temple Dedication 5:11-14

12 and all the Levitical singers, Asaph, Heman, Jeduthun, and their sons and kinsmen, clothed in fine linen, with cymbals, harps, and lyres, standing east of the altar, and with them one hundred and twenty priests blowing trumpets
13 in unison when the trumpeters and the singers were to make themselves heard with one voice to praise and to glorify the LORD, and when they lifted up their voice accompa-

2 Chronicles

nied by trumpets and cymbals and instruments of music, and when they praised the LORD *saying,* "*He* indeed is good for His lovingkindness is everlasting," then the house, the house of the LORD, was filled with a cloud,

This marks the moving of the ark of the covenant from where David had placed it when he recovered the ark from the Philistines to the temple that Solomon had built. It is finally brought to its permanent place.

This was one large orchestra and choir. Although only the number of trumpeters (120) is given, we can assume that there were 288 singers plus all the other instrumentalists who played the cymbals, harps, and lyres. Having rehearsed their music, they were to play and sing in unison. In our worship the one activity that is the most united of all is music. When we sing or play, we sing the same melody, the same rhythm, the same harmony, the same words and the same dynamics.

The purpose of rehearsal is to have the musicians conform to the wishes of the conductor. Until the conductor has that united conformity, the performance cannot be considered to be of the quality that we expect. In our world of individuality this is still one activity that cannot function without the absolute conformity demanded by a professional conductor of music. And only when these instruments and musicians are dedicated to the service of the Lord can they be at their ultimate in the function that God intended.

Solomon's Sacrifices 7:4-7

6 And the priests stood at their posts and the Levites, with the instruments of music to the LORD, which King David had made for giving praise to the LORD—"for His lovingkindness is everlasting"—whenever he gave praise by their means, while the priests on the other side blew trumpets; and all Israel was standing.

2 Chronicles

In the previous passage the account indicates that so many sheep and oxen were sacrificed that they could not be numbered (5:6). In this account, after Solomon had prayed, 22,000 oxen and 120,000 sheep were sacrificed.

The music of the Levites was very focused in its purpose: to praise the Lord. In this case the music was antiphonal: the instruments of music, whatever they were, were on one side and the priests with the trumpets were on the other side. Not only was this event of grand proportions, it was also of considerable length, seven days.

Solomon and the Queen of Sheba 9:1-12

11 And from the algum the king made steps for the house of the Lord and for the king's palace, and lyres and harps for the singers; and none like that was seen before in the land of Judah.

The algum trees, sometimes also simply called almug, brought by the Queen of Sheba served two purposes. It was used to build the steps leading up to the temple and for some of the instruments, especially harps and lyres. One of its properties must be its hardness for it to be used in a heavy traffic area such as steps. Second, it must provide good resonance to make it preferable as a wood for these instruments. It was obviously a new wood to the Israelites since it is noted that this had not been seen before in the land of Judah. If it is, as thought by some to be, sandalwood, then the wood is white and shiny and has a pleasant odor when burned.

Abijah Exhorts Israel 13:4-12

12 "Now behold, God is with us at *our* head and His priests with the signal trumpets to sound the alarm against you. O sons of Israel, do not fight against the Lord God of your fathers, for you will not succeed."

2 Chronicles

Here is another example of the trumpets *(chatsotsrah)* being used as a signal in war, with the priests in the battle to blow them as they did in the taking of Jericho.

Israel and Judah at War 13:13-20

14 When Judah turned around, behold, they were attacked both front and rear; so they cried to the LORD, and the priests blew the trumpets.

It was as the people of Judah predicted, the Lord would be with Israel and at the sound of the war trumpets *(chatsotsrah)*, the army would be routed.

Asa Removes Idols 15:8-15

14 Moreover, they made an oath to the LORD with a loud voice, with shouting, with trumpets, and with horns.

Two types of blown instruments are listed here. The first is the straight trumpet *(chatsotsrah)* usually used in war and the second is the crooked trumpet *(shofar)*, here translated horns.

Jehoshaphat at War 20:20-30

21 And when he had consulted with the people, he appointed those who sang to the LORD and those who praised *Him* in holy attire, as they went out before the army and said, "Give thanks to the LORD, for His lovingkindness is everlasting."

22 And when they began singing and praising, the LORD set ambushes against the sons of Ammon, Moab, and Mount Seir, who had come against Judah; so they were routed.

28 And they came to Jerusalem with harps, lyres, and trumpets to the house of the LORD.

Here is another example of very unorthodox battle strategy. The musicians are requested to come to the battlefields where they begin singing praises. Then God sets ambushes, defeating the sons of Ammon and Moab without the people of Judah even

2 Chronicles

entering into battle. To use musicians to actually fight the war is seldom considered today. But then, God is also seldom given the credit for winning a war once the mission has been accomplished.

It appears that more than trumpets and singers were involved in the battle because when they returned they also came with harps *(kinnor)* and lyres *(nebhel)*.

Athaliah Killed 23:12-21

13 And she looked, and behold, the king was standing by his pillar at the entrance, and the captains and the trumpeters *were* beside the king. And all the people of the land rejoiced and blew trumpets, the singers with *their* musical instruments leading the praise. Then Athaliah tore her clothes and said, "Treason! Treason!"

This is an instance where the priest, in this case Jehoiada, took control of a serious situation and strengthened himself to make it possible to crown young Joash king. This meant that, first of all, they needed to be rid of the queen and, secondly, that young Joash needed to be crowned. This was done with great pomp and ceremony with the blowing of the straight trumpets *(chatsotsrah)*. In addition, the singers with their instruments *(keli)* led the praise.

Jehoida Renounces Baal 23:16-21

18 Moreover, Jehoiada placed the offices of the house of the LORD under the authority of the Levitical priests, whom David had assigned over the house of the LORD, to offer the burnt offerings of the LORD, as it is written in the law of Moses—with rejoicing and singing according to the order of David.

Jehoiada was not about to leave this task half done. Baal idols were destroyed. Mattan the priest of Baal was killed. The

2 Chronicles

ministry of the Levites was revitalized. Singing and rejoicing according to the order of David was reinstituted. Gatekeepers and captains were reassigned. As a result the land rejoiced and the city was quiet.

Hezekiah Sacrifices and Worships 29:20-36

25 He then stationed the Levites in the house of the LORD with cymbals, with harps, and with lyres, according to the command of David and of Gad the king's seer, and of Nathan the prophet; for the command was from the LORD through His prophets.

26 And the Levites stood with the *musical* instruments of David, and the priests with the trumpets.

27 Then Hezekiah gave the order to offer the burnt offering on the altar. When the burnt offering began, the song to the LORD also began with the trumpets, *accompanied* by the instruments of David, king of Israel.

28 While the whole assembly worshiped, the singers also sang and the trumpets sounded; all this *continued* until the burnt offering was finished.

30 Moreover, King Hezekiah and the officials ordered the Levites to sing praises to the LORD with the words of David and Asaph the seer. So they sang praises with joy, and bowed down and worshipped.

Again and again the Israelites strayed from the Lord. King Ahaz had gone to the extent of destroying a portion of the temple and also some of the utensils. When Hezekiah ascended to the throne he restored the temple worship. This passage recounts the celebration on that occasion. Cymbals *(metsiltayim)*, harps *(nebhel)*, lyres *(kinnor)* and trumpets *(chatsotsrah)* were in use.

These and other instruments were accompanied by singing. This music was offered to the Lord also as an accompaniment to the sacrifices that were brought as the people consecrated

2 Chronicles

themselves to the Lord again. From the moment that the sacrifice began, the music started and continued until the sacrifice was complete. The idea of an offertory certainly is not one that we discovered only in recent church practice.

Feast of Unleavened Bread 30:13-22
21 And the sons of Israel present in Jerusalem celebrated the Feast of Unleavened Bread *for* seven days with great joy, and the Levites and the priests praised the LORD day after day with loud instruments to the LORD.

Loud instruments occur on more than one occasion in the Scriptures, this being one of them. We might argue that it would be all right to have loudness occasionally, and in certain sections of music to provide for expressiveness not otherwise possible. But this verse seems to suggest that the volume was fairly relentless because we are told that the priests praised the Lord day after day with loud instruments. In fact if we take this literally, they played this music for seven days, the whole time allotted to the Feast of Unleavened Bread. Woodstock and Cornerstone move over.

Temple Repair 34:8-13
12 And the men did the work faithfully with foremen over them to supervise: Jahath and Obadiah, the Levites of the sons of Merari, Zechariah and Meshullam of the sons of the Kohathites, and the Levites, all who were skillful with musical instruments.

It is not clear how the Levites who were skillful with instruments were involved in the reconstruction of the temple and it's edifices, but presumably they were part of the supervisory team for the project. Being musicians did not exclude them from roles that would seem to have gone to others who might have specialized in construction.

2 Chronicles-Ezra

The Passover 35:10-15

15 The singers, the sons of Asaph, *were* also at their stations according to the command of David, Asaph, Heman, and Jeduthun the king's seer; and the gatekeepers at each gate did not have to depart from their service, because the Levites their brethren prepared for them.

Lament for Josiah 35:20-27

25 Then Jeremiah chanted a lament for Josiah. And all the male and female singers speak about Josiah in their lamentations to this day. And they made them an ordinance in Israel; behold, they are also written in the Lamentations.

In the Old Testament, lamentations *(qinah)* were a significant aspect in sorrowing for a great leader. David lamented the deaths of Saul and Jonathan (2 Samuel 1:19-27) in a song that celebrated their lives and accomplishments. These compositions were the obituaries of the time and provided a vehicle for both honor and sorrow.

Ezra

Return from Exile 2:1-70

41 The singers: the sons of Asaph, 128.

65 besides their male and female servants, who numbered 7,337; and they had 200 singing men and women.

70 Now the priests and the Levites, some of the people, the singers, the gatekeepers, and the temple servants lived in their cities, and all Israel in their cities.

According to 1 Chronicles 23:5 David had four thousand who praised the Lord with instruments. When this ragtag group of Israelites returned from the exile, only two hundred singers were numbered in the census. The once massive choir and

Ezra

orchestra that had served in the temple had been decimated to a relatively small contingent. The once highly developed musical establishment had become a mere vestige of its former glorious splendor. One can imagine how minuscule the choir must have seemed to those who remembered the majesty of the former days.

Rejoicing over Temple Rebuilding 3:8-13

10 Now when the builders had laid the foundation of the temple of the LORD, the priests stood in their apparel with trumpets, and the Levites, the sons of Asaph, with cymbals, to praise the LORD according to the directions of King David of Israel.

11 And they sang, praising and giving thanks to the LORD, *saying,* "For He is good, for His lovingkindness is upon Israel forever." And all the people shouted with a great shout when they praised the LORD because the foundation of the house of the LORD was laid.

After a considerable time they finally got to the rebuilding of the temple. The laying of the foundation of a building was a time for celebration, and that was certainly the case here, but it was bittersweet, especially for the older ones who had seen the splendor of the first temple. This second one, although cause for rejoicing, did not compare. There were shouts of joy from some but weeping from others.

Ezra and Exiles Return 7:1-10

7 And some of the sons of Israel and some of the priests, the Levites, the singers, the gatekeepers, and the temple servants went up to Jerusalem in the seventh year of King Artaxerxes.

Tax Laws 7:11-26

24 We also inform you that it is not allowed to impose tax, tribute or toll *on* any of the priests, Levites, singers, doorkeepers, Nethinim, or servants of this house of God.

Ezra-Nehemiah

In the service of the temple God had instructed that the Levitical tribe would not own land, nor would they be required to pay taxes. Here a decree from Artaxerxes, a godless king, confirms this arrangement for the new temple service.

Marriage to Foreign Women 10:18-24

24 And of the singers *there was* Eliashib; and of the gatekeepers: Shallum, Telem, and Uri.

The singers transgressed, as had others.

Nehemiah

Rebuilding of the Wall 4:15-23

18 As for the builders, each *wore* his sword girded at his side as he built, while the trumpeter *stood* near me.

20 "At whatever place you hear the sound of the trumpet, rally to us there. Our God will fight for us."

The crooked trumpet *(shofar)*, which was frequently used in the temple festivities, is here the instrument of choice to warn of the enemy. To Nehemiah, the task of rebuilding the wall and the temple was a holy task and was one where God was also at work, defending and fighting for them if necessary. The sharp, biting blast of this instrument would serve well to alert all to rally to the defense of the city.

Appointed Singers 7:1-73

1 Now it came about when the wall was rebuilt and I had set up the doors, and the gatekeepers and the singers and the Levites were appointed,

44 The singers: the sons of Asaph, 148.

67 besides their male and their female servants, of whom *there were* 7,337; and they had 245 male and female singers.

Nehemiah

73 Now the priests, the Levites, the gatekeepers, the singers, some of the people, the temple servants, and all Israel, lived in their cities.

The number of singers is somewhat at variance with the number given in Ezra 2:65, but it is quite possible that when taken chronologically, there were different numbers at different times as the people came back. The final number given here is actually 245 rather than the 200 mentioned in Ezra. In any case, the number is very small compared to the pre-exilic choir. As in Ezra, it is noted that there were men and women singers.

Dedication to God's Service 10:28-31

28 Now the rest of the people, the priests, the Levites, the gatekeepers, the singers, the temple servants, and all those who had separated themselves from the peoples of the lands to the law of God, their wives, their sons and their daughters, all those who had knowledge and understanding,

Nehemiah, the governor, and Ezra, the priest, were concerned about much more than rebuilding the wall and the temple. They knew that the people needed revival of the heart much more desperately than they needed a refurbishing of the physical condition of the city. Because of this need they led them through a reading of the Word of God which had been neglected for so long. As they discovered what the Lord had commanded, the people began to obey instructions, such as the proclaiming of festivals to celebrate God.

The singers were a part of these events and followed the instructions just like the others. They took the solemn oath which stated that they would (1) keep and observe God's commandments, ordinances, and statutes; (2) not exchange daughters with the people of the land; (3) not buy and sell on the Sabbath day; (4) forgo the crops of the seventh year; (5) forgo

Nehemiah

the repayment of debts; (6) annually contribute one-third of a shekel to the temple service; (7) provide wood for the temple; (8) bring the first-born of sons and cattle; and (9) tithe of the products of the land.

Support for the Levites 10:34-39

39 For the sons of Israel and the sons of Levi shall bring the contribution of the grain, the new wine and the oil, to the chambers; there are the utensils of the sanctuary, the priests who are ministering, the gatekeepers, and the singers. Thus we will not neglect the house of our God.

Because the people contributed to the sanctuary, the house of the Lord was not neglected.

Levite Overseers 11:22-24

22 Now the overseer of the Levites in Jerusalem was Uzzi the son of Bani, the son of Hashabiah, the son of Mattaniah, the son of Mica, from the sons of Asaph, who were the singers for the service of the house of God.
23 For *there was* a commandment from the king concerning them and a firm regulation for the song leaders day by day.

What this firm regulation was, we don't know. It's possible that it was simply a schedule that determined when the singers were to be on duty. The "day by day" phrase seems to suggest this.

Priests and Levites 12:1-8

8 And the Levites *were* Jeshua, Binnui, Kadmiel, Sherebiah, Judah, *and* Mattaniah *who was* in charge of the songs of thanksgiving, he and his brothers.

Dedication of the Wall 12:27-47

27 Now at the dedication of the wall of Jerusalem they sought out the Levites from all their places, to bring them to Jerusalem so that they might celebrate the dedication with

Nehemiah

gladness, with hymns of thanksgiving and with songs *to the accompaniment* of cymbals, harps, and lyres.

28 So the sons of the singers were assembled from the district around Jerusalem, and from the villages of the Netophathites,

29 from Beth-gilgal, and from *their* fields in Geba and Azmaveth, for the singers had built themselves villages around Jerusalem.

31 Then I had the leaders of Judah come up on top of the wall, and I appointed two great choirs, the first proceeding to the right on top of the wall toward the Refuse Gate.

35 and some of the sons of the priests with trumpets; *and* Zechariah the son of Jonathan, the son of Shemaiah, the son of Mattaniah, the son of Micaiah, the son of Zaccur, the son of Asaph,

36 and his kinsmen, Shemaiah, Azarel, Milalai, Gilalai, Maai, Nethanel, Judah *and* Hanani, with the musical instruments of David the man of God. And Ezra the scribe went before them.

38 The second choir proceeded to the left, while I followed them with half of the people on the wall, above the Tower of Furnaces, to the Broad Wall,

40 Then the two choirs took their stand in the house of God. So did I and half of the officials with me;

41 and the priests, Eliakim, Maaseiah, Miniamin, Micaiah, Elioenai, Zechariah, and Hananiah, with the trumpets;

42 and Maaseiah, Shemaiah, Eleazar, Uzzi, Jehohanan, Malchijah, Elam, and Ezer. And the singers sang, with Jezrahiah *their* leader,

45 For they performed the worship of their God and the service of purification, together with the singers and the gatekeepers in accordance with the command of David *and* of his son Solomon.

Nehemiah

46 For in the days of David and Asaph, in ancient times, *there were* leaders of the singers, songs of praise and hymns of thanksgiving to God.

47 And so all Israel in the days of Zerubbabel and Nehemiah gave the portions due the singers and the gatekeepers as each day required, and set apart the consecrated *portion* for the Levites, and the Levites set apart the consecrated *portion* for the sons of Aaron.

This was only the dedication of the wall, but Nehemiah made it a celebration that rivaled that of previous military celebrations, the Red Sea deliverance dance, and the dedication of the first temple.

This event brought together all the musicians of the tribe of Levi: singers, trumpeters, percussionists, string players, and other instrumentalists playing what are here, and in other passages, called the instruments of David. They were to sing hymns of praise and songs of thanksgiving.

The singers were divided into two antiphonal choirs that formed processionals along the wall with the temple as the destination. This musical spectacle caused emotions to well up among the people that made even the women and children to rejoice. Throughout this account it is emphasized that the emotions of the day were thanksgiving, gladness and joy.

Since the Levites were trained performers, the worship is described as a performance of worship, a concept that is not common in the Bible. Whatever was included in the service, it was what had been commanded by David and Solomon.

A notable conclusion to this account is the reiteration that during the days of Zerubbabel and Nehemiah the singers and other Levites were given the portions due them.

Support Neglected 13:4-14

5 had prepared a large room for him, where formerly they put the grain offerings, the frankincense, the utensils, and

Nehemiah-Job

the tithes of grain, wine and oil prescribed for the Levites, the singers and the gatekeepers, and the contributions for the priests.

10 I also discovered that the portions of the Levites had not been given *them,* so that the Levites and the singers who performed the service had gone away, each to his own field.

Sin had entered the camp.

Esther

There are no references to music in the Book of Esther.

Job

The Prosperity of the Wicked 21:1-16
12 "They sing to the timbrel and harp
And rejoice at the sound of the flute.

This verse is included as an indication of the pleasures enjoyed by the wicked, who, as far as Job can tell, are prospering, and in addition to the pleasures of music, have their offspring nearby, have safe houses, have mating animals, plus other domestic delights. Not only that, but the people have told God to get out of their lives.

As a commentary on music, this verse again indicates that singing was often accompanied by instruments. The timbrel *(toph),* a hand drum, and the harp would have provided a sparse but adequate accompaniment.

Job Desires Past Glory 29:1-25
13 "The blessing of the one ready to perish

Job

came upon me,
And I made the widow's heart sing for joy.

As Job is reminiscing about his past life, he recalls his children, his friendship with God, the awe he was given by younger men, and the way he had helped those weaker than he. One of the results of serving others, he remembers, is that it caused the widow's heart to sing for joy. He longs for those days of ministry.

Reasons for Sorrow 30:24-31
31 "Therefore my harp is turned to mourning,
And my flute to the sound of those who weep.

Job lists many reasons why, if the world or life were fair, he should be having a pleasant, fulfilling life. For music to be sad or sorrowful is possibly the most poignant commentary on the state of a person who has been known mostly as a successful and positive person. For Job these instruments had been instruments of joy, but now the harp *(kinnor)* and the flute *(uggab)* (in some translations the *organ*) had turned to mourning and weeping.

It could also be argued that since music is the medium most suited to express the deepest feelings of joy, it is also the medium that is most appropriate for expressing the deepest agonies. No doubt the composers of opera would say that music adds a dimension that makes the expression of the deepest pathos possible that words only could not achieve.

The Work of an Angel 33:23-28
27 "He will sing to men and say,
I have sinned and perverted what is right,
And it is not proper for me.

Man's Cries to God 35:9-16
10 "But no one says, 'Where is God my Maker,

Job

Who gives songs in the night,

Who gets the credit for the joy we experience in the evening, in the night, in the morning? These joys are usually credited to humanity's own personal accomplishments and undeserved genetic or circumstantial gifts. But we need to recognize the source of that joy as God.

God's Magnificence 36:24-33
24 "Remember that you should exalt His work,
Of which men have sung.

God Questions Job 38:1-7
7 When the morning stars sang together,
And all the sons of God shouted for joy?

God is quizzing Job about creation to impress on him that it was God who was there when it all flew into empty space. This beautiful picture of rejoicing at creation has the stars singing and the angels (the sons of God) shouting. God was not alone; He had His cheering section. It was music that was used to celebrate this major event. But Job needed to realize that he was created and was not there when God began the universe.

To celebrate this we need music. Haydn tried to do this by writing "The Creation" and succeeded remarkably in demonstrating its grandeur and intimacy. The three narrators, Adam, Eve, and Gabriel, combined with the choir and orchestra are able to provide these contrasts in very moving passages.

God Questions Job 39:19-25
24 "With shaking and rage
he races over the ground;
And he does not stand still
at the voice of the trumpet.
25 "As often as the trumpet *sounds*
he says, "Aha!"

> And he scents the battle from afar,
> And thunder of the captains,
> and the war cry.

The Psalms

The psalms are poetry contributions from various authors, not only King David, as is often thought. Other authors are the sons of Korah, Asaph, Solomon, Heman, Ethan, Moses, as well as many anonymous writers. These poetic writings form the hymnbook of biblical times with each psalm being a potential song text.

The meaning of the word *psalm* can be simply given as "a poem to be sung (possibly with an instrument)." The title for this book, which we call the Psalms, in Hebrew is Book of Hymns or Praises.

It should be noted here that Hebrew poetry follows other forms and patterns than we are used to, certainly in our hymn poetry. The lines do not rhyme, even in the Hebrew. The most common technique of the poets is to utilize couplets that are related by the ideas they express rather than by words that rhyme. The couplets might express similar ideas where the second line will elaborate on the idea of the first one or the two lines will express opposite ideas to emphasize a point.

Other techniques include the use of acrostics, as in Psalm 119 where each set of eight verses begins with a successive letter of the Hebrew alphabet. A few Psalms, such as 136, alternate a new idea with a refrain that repeats throughout the 26 verses.

The superscriptions of the Psalms are in the Hebrew text. Because of this, and because of the insights they provide, they are included in this compilation. The superscriptions are of several types: (1) they give historical contexts, (2) they give specific musical instructions, (3) they indicate for whom psalms were written, and (4) they indicate by whom they were written.

Psalms

Not all of the Psalms have these superscriptions. Many have nothing; presumably whatever instructions there might have been were passed on orally and, sometime over the years, were lost. In the following comments, as each new term occurs, explanations will be suggested.

It should also be noted that the Book of Psalms is divided into five books, each of which ends with a doxology:

Book 1   Psalms 1-41
Book 2   Psalms 42-72
Book 3   Psalms 73-89
Book 4   Psalms 90-106
Book 5   Psalms 107-150

Superscription 3:0
A Psalm of David, when he fled from Absalom his son.

Selah 3:2, 4, 8

The term *selah* is considered a musical term by most authorities and is therefore included as such. The term appears seventy-three times in the Psalms and three times in Habakkuk. The musical meanings that have been suggested include concepts such as modulation, repetition, metric change, a rest, or a change of tone.

Selah has also been defined as an instruction to consider what has just been said, something like "meditate on this for a while" or "weigh this." But it must be admitted that we cannot conclusively define this word that so often occurs in the Psalms.

Superscription 4:0
For the choir director; on stringed instruments.
A Psalm of David.

On *Neginoth*, which is here translated "on stringed instruments," also occurs in the superscription of Psalms 6, 54, 55, 61, and 76.

61

Psalms

Selah 4:2, 4

Superscription 5:0
For the choir director; for flute accompaniment.
A Psalm of David.

On *Nehiloth* is an obscure term and its translation involves considerable speculation. This translation renders it as "for flute accompaniment."

Joy in God's Shelter 5:11, 12
11 But let all who take refuge in Thee be glad,
Let them ever sing for joy;
And mayest Thou shelter them,
That those who love Thy name may exult in Thee.

Superscription 6:0
For the choir director; with stringed instruments, upon an eight-stringed lyre. A Psalm of David.

A new term, *Sheminith,* is here translated "upon an eight-stringed lyre."

Superscription 7:0
A Shiggaion of David, which he sang to the LORD concerning Cush, a Benjamite.

The New American Standard Bible translates the term *Shiggaion* as dithyrambic rhythm or wild, passionate song.

Selah 7:5

Praise and Thanksgiving 7:17
17 I will give thanks to the LORD according to
His righteousness,
And will sing praise to the name of the
LORD Most High.

Psalms

Certainly the singing of praises is the most common instruction given in the Scriptures as it relates to worshipping God. Our present-day hymns give us a variety of subjects or focuses. Some are addressed to God in praise as this psalm instructs, but many others are addressed to people. The psalms could be categorized as to whether they are addressed to God or to people.

The history of hymn singing shows that the pendulum often swings from one extreme to the other. The British hymn of Watts's time tended to be addressed to God while the American gospel song of the nineteenth century tended to address the people in exhortation. Both are necessary and it is our task as musicians to see that both are represented in the hymn singing of the church.

It has also been suggested that all the psalms can be put in a grid that places personal and corporate on one side and intersects with positive and negative on the other as follows:

	POSITIVE	NEGATIVE
PERSONAL		
CORPORATE		

Within this grid a psalm could, for example, be a personal psalm using the pronoun "I" and express negative feelings to either God or people or both. An example of such a psalm would be Psalm 13. Or a psalm might indicate positive thoughts in a corporate expression using the pronoun "we." Other psalms would fall into a different quadrant depending on the subject material.

Superscription 8:0
For the choir director; on the Gittith.
A Psalm of David.

The *Gittith* appears to be an instrument, but we don't know what it might have been.

Psalms

Superscription 9:0
For the choir director; on Muth-labben. A Psalm of David.

As is the case with many of the superscription terms, this one has a literal meaning, "upon death to a son." It is thought that there is a musical meaning likely indicating a type of musical instrument.

Praise and Thanksgiving 9:1, 2
2 I will be glad and exult in Thee;
I will sing praise to Thy name, O Most High.

Praise 9:11-16
11 Sing praises to the LORD,
who dwells in Zion;
Declare among the peoples His deeds.

Selah 9:16, 20

Superscription 11:0
For the choir director. A *Psalm* of David.

Superscription 12:0
For the choir director; upon an eight-stringed lyre. A Psalm of David.

Superscription 13:0
For the choir director. A Psalm of David.

Praise 13:5, 6
6 I will sing to the LORD,
Because He has dealt bountifully with me.

Superscription 14:0
For the choir director. A *Psalm* of David.

Superscription 15:0
A Psalm of David.

Psalms

Superscription 16:0
A Mikhtam of David.

A *Mikhtam* is possibly another word for psalm or, as the NASB indicates in the footnote, an "Epigrammatic Poem or Atonement Psalm."

Superscription 17:0
A Prayer of David.

Superscription 18:0
For the choir director. A *Psalm* of David the servant of the Lord, who spoke to the Lord the words of this song in the day that the Lord delivered him from the hand of all his enemies and from the hand of Saul. And he said,

Praise and Thanksgiving 18:46-50
49 Therefore I will give thanks to Thee among
the nations, O Lord,
And I will sing praises to Thy name.

Superscription 19:0
For the choir director. A Psalm of David.

Superscription 20:0
For the choir director. A Psalm of David.

Selah 20:3

Superscription 21:0
For the choir director. A Psalm of David.

Selah 21:2

Praise 21:7-13
13 Be Thou exalted, O Lord, in Thy strength;
We will sing and praise Thy power.

Psalms

Superscription 22:0
For the choir director; upon Aijeleth Hashshahar.
A Psalm of David.

Since the literal meaning of *Aijeleth Hashshahar* is "the hind of the morning," it is possible that this could mean that the psalm is to be sung to the tune that is known by this phrase.

Superscription 23:0
A Psalm of David.

Superscription 24:0
A Psalm of David.

Selah 24:6, 10

Superscription 25:0
A *Psalm* of David.

Superscription 26:0
A *Psalm* of David.

Superscription 27:0
A *Psalm* of David.

Temple Worship 27:4-6
6 And now my head will be lifted up above my
enemies around me;
And I will offer in His tent sacrifices with
shouts of joy;
I will sing, yes, I will sing praises
to the LORD.

Superscription 28:0
A *Psalm* of David.

Thanksgiving 28:6-9
7 The LORD is my strength and my shield;
My heart trusts in Him, and I am helped;

Psalms

Therefore my heart exults,
And with my song I shall thank Him.

Superscription 29:0
A Psalm of David

Superscription 30:0
A Psalm;
a Song at the Dedication of the House.
A *Psalm* of David.

Praise and Thanksgiving 30:1-5
4 Sing praise to the LORD, you His godly ones,
And give thanks to His holy name.

Praise and Thanksgiving 30:10-12
11 Thou hast turned for me my mourning
into dancing;
Thou hast loosed my sackcloth and girded
me with gladness;
12 That *my* soul may sing praise to Thee, and
not be silent.
O LORD my God, I will give thanks to Thee forever.

Superscription 31:0
For the choir director.
A Psalm of David.

Superscription32:0
A *Psalm* of David. A Maskil.

The term *maskil* is found in Psalms 32, 42, 44, 45, 52, 53, 54, 55, 74, 78, 88, 89, 142. Although the immediate meaning is "poem" or "song," scholars have concluded that it also suggests this is a didactic or teaching psalm.

Confession of Sin 32:3-7
7 Thou art my hiding place;

Psalms

Thou dost preserve me from trouble;
Thou dost surround me with songs of deliverance.

Selah 32: 4,5, 7

Praise and Thanksgiving 33:1-5
1 Sing for joy in the LORD,
O you righteous ones;
Praise is becoming to the upright.
2 Give thanks to the LORD with the lyre;
Sing praises to Him with a harp of ten strings.
3 Sing to Him a new song;
Play skillfully with a shout of joy.

This passage is an illustration of the use of several Hebrew words to indicate singing. In verse 1 *ranan* introduces the "singing" motif running through the first five verses. The other two words used are *zamar* in verse 2 and the more common *shir* in verse 3. Verse 3 also includes the exhortation to play skillfully *(yatab)*.

Superscription 34:0
A *Psalm* of David when he feigned madness before Abimelech, who drove him away and he departed.

Superscription 35:0
A *Psalm* of David.

Superscription 36:0
For the choir director.
A *Psalm* of David the servant of the LORD.

Superscription 37:0
A *Psalm* of David.

Psalms

Superscription 38:0
A Psalm of David, for a memorial.

Superscription 39:0
For the choir director, for Jeduthun. A Psalm of David.

Selah 39:5, 11

Superscription 40:0
For the choir director. A Psalm of David.

Praise for Deliverance 40:1-3
3 And He put a new song in my mouth, a song
of praise to our God;
Many will see and fear,
And will trust in the LORD.

Superscription 41:0
For the choir director. A Psalm of David.

Superscription 42:0
For the choir director. A Maskil of the sons of Korah.

God's Presence in Despair 42:5-8
8 The LORD will command His lovingkindness
in the daytime;
And His song will be with me in the night,
A prayer to the God of my life.

Praise and Offerings 43:1-4
4 Then I will go to the altar of God,
To God my exceeding joy;
And upon the lyre I shall praise Thee, O
God, my God.

Superscription 44:0
For the choir director. A Maskil of the sons of Korah.

Psalms

Selah 44:8

Superscription 45:0

For the choir director; according to the Shoshannim. A Maskil of the sons of Korah. A Song of Love.

Shoshannim literally means "lily" but could also refer to an instrument shaped like a lily.

God's Eternal Throne 45:6-9

8 All Thy garments are *fragrant with* myrrh
and aloes *and* cassia;
Out of ivory palaces stringed instruments
have made Thee glad.

Superscription 46:0

For the choir director. A *Psalm* of the sons of Korah, set to Alamoth. A Song.

Alamoth probably refers to treble voices.

Selah 46:3, 7, 11

Superscription 47:0

For the choir director. A Psalm of the sons of Korah.

Selah 47:4

Praise 47:5-9

5 God has ascended with a shout,
The LORD, with the sound of a trumpet.
6 Sing praises to God, sing praises;
Sing praises to our King, sing praises.
7 For God is the King of all the earth;
Sing praises with a skillful psalm.

Superscription 48:0

A Song; a Psalm of the sons of Korah.

Psalms

Selah 48:8

Superscription 49:0
For the choir director. A Psalm of the sons of Korah.

A Witness to All Peoples 49:1-4
4 I will incline my ear to a proverb;
I will express my riddle on the harp.

Selah 49:13, 15

Superscription 50:0
A Psalm of Asaph.

Selah 50:6

Superscription 51:0
For the choir director. A Psalm of David, when Nathan the prophet came to him, after he had gone in to Bathsheba.

Sacrifices and Forgiveness 51:14-17
14 Deliver me from bloodguiltiness, O God,
Thou God of my salvation;
Then my tongue will joyfully sing of Thy
righteousness.

Superscription 52:0
For the choir director. A Maskil of David, when Doeg the Edomite came and told Saul, and said to him, "David has come to the house of Ahimelech."

Selah 52:3, 5

Superscription 53:0
For the choir director; according to Mahalath. A Maskil of David.

Mahalath refers to sickness or possibly a sad tone.

Psalms

Superscription 54:0

For the choir director; on stringed instruments. A Maskil of David, when the Ziphites came and said to Saul, "Is not David hiding himself among us?"

Selah 54:3

Superscription 55:0

For the choir director; on stringed instruments. A Maskil of David.

Selah 55:7, 19

Superscription 56:0

For the choir director; according to Jonath elem rehokim. A *Mikhtam* of David, when the Philistines seized him in Gath.

Superscription 57:0

For the choir director; *set to* Al-tashheth. A Mikhtam of David, when he fled from Saul, in the cave.

Al-tashheth means "do not destroy" and could also, as in other titles, indicate a tune to which the psalm was to be sung.

Selah 57:3, 6
Praise and Thanksgiving 57:7-11
7 My heart is steadfast, O God, my heart is
steadfast;
I will sing, yes, I will sing praises!
8 Awake, my glory;
Awake, harp and lyre,
I will awaken the dawn!
9 I will give thanks to Thee, O Lord, among
the peoples;
I will sing praises to Thee among
the nations.

Psalms

Superscription 58:0

For the choir director; *set to* Al-tashheth. A Mikhtam of David.

Superscription 59:0

For the choir director; *set to* Al-tashheth. A Mikhtam of David, when Saul sent *men*, and they watched the house in order to kill him.

Selah 59:5, 13

Praise 59:16, 17

16 But as for me, I shall sing of Thy strength;
Yes, I shall joyfully sing of Thy lovingkindness in the morning,
For Thou hast been my stronghold,
And a refuge in the day of my distress.
17 O my strength, I will sing praises to Thee;
For God is my stronghold, the God who
shows me lovingkindness.

Superscription 60:0

For the choir director; according to Shushan Eduth. A Mikhtam of David, to teach; when he struggled with Aram-naharaim and with Aram-zobah, and Joab returned, and smote twelve thousand of Edom in the Valley of Salt.

Shushan Eduth, meaning " the lily of the testimony," could signify either a lily-shaped instrument or a melody.

Selah 60:4

Superscription 61:0

For the choir director, on a stringed instrument. A *Psalm* of David.

Selah 61:4

Praise for the King's Longevity 61:5-8
8 So I will sing praise to Thy name forever,

Psalms

That I may pay my vows day by day.

Superscription 62:0
For the choir director; according to Jeduthun. A Psalm of David.

Selah 62:4, 8

Superscription 63:0
A Psalm of David, when he was in the wilderness of Judah.

Clinging to God 63:6-8
7 For Thou hast been my help,
And in the shadow of Thy wings I sing for joy.

Superscription 64:0
For the choir director. A Psalm of David.

Superscription 65:0
For the choir director. A Psalm of David. A Song.

God in Nature 65:9-13
13 The meadows are clothed with flocks,
And the valleys are covered with grain;
They shout for joy, yes, they sing.

Superscription 66:0
For the choir director. A Song. A Psalm.

Praise for God's Greatness 66:1-4
2 Sing the glory of His name;
Make His praise glorious.

4 "All the earth will worship Thee,
And will sing praises to Thee;
They will sing praises to Thy name."

Selah 66:4, 7, 15

Psalms

Superscription 67:0
For the choir director; with stringed instruments. A Psalm. A Song.

Selah 67:1, 4

Praise 67:1-7
4 Let the nations be glad and sing for joy;
For Thou wilt judge the peoples
with uprightness,
And guide the nations on the earth.

Superscription 68:0
For the choir director. A Psalm of David. A Song.

Praise 68:1-4
4 Sing to God, sing praises to His name;
Cast up *a*
highway for Him
who rides through the deserts,
Whose name is the LORD,
and exult before Him.

Selah 68:7, 19, 32

Temple Worship 68:24-27
25 The singers went on,
the musicians after *them*,
In the midst of the maidens
beating tambourines.

The term for beating is *tapheph*, meaning "to sound the timbrel, beat."

God's Majesty 68:32-35
32 Sing to God, O kingdoms of the earth;
Sing praises to the Lord,

Psalms

Superscription 69:0
For the choir director; according to Shoshannim. A *Psalm* of David.

Derision by Enemies 69:5-12
12 Those who sit in the gate talk about me,
And I *am* the song of the drunkards.

Resolution to Praise 69:29-33
30 I will praise the name of God with song,
And shall magnify Him with thanksgiving.

Superscription 70:0
For the choir director. A *Psalm* of David; for a memorial.

Praise to God 71:22-24
22 I will also praise Thee with a harp,
Even Thy truth, O my God;
To Thee I will sing praises with the lyre,
O Thou Holy One of Israel.
23 My lips will shout for joy when I sing praises
to Thee;
And my soul, which Thou hast redeemed.

Superscription 72:0
A *Psalm* of Solomon.

Superscription 73:0
A Psalm of Asaph.

Superscription 74:0
A Maskil of Asaph.

Superscription 75:0
For the choir director; *set to* Al-tashheth. A Psalm of Asaph, a Song.

Selah 75:3

Psalms

Praise to God 75:9

9 But as for me, I will declare *it* forever;
I will sing praises to the God of Jacob.

Superscription 76:0

For the choir director; on stringed instruments. A Psalm of Asaph, a Song.

Selah 76:3, 9

Superscription 77:0

For the choir director; according to Jeduthun. A Psalm of Asaph.

Selah 77:3, 9, 15

Anguish in Trouble 77:1-6

6 I will remember my song in the night;
I will meditate with my heart;
And my spirit ponders.

Superscription 78:0

A Maskil of Asaph.

Israel's Rebellion 78:54-64

63 Fire devoured His young men;
And His virgins had no wedding songs.

Superscription 79:0

A Psalm of Asaph.

Superscription 80:0

For the choir director; *set to* El Shoshannim; Eduth. A Psalm of Asaph.

Superscription 81:0

For the choir director; on the Gittith. A *Psalm* of Asaph.

Psalms

Rejoicing 81:1-5
1 Sing for joy to God our strength;
Shout joyfully to the God of Jacob.
2 Raise a song, strike the timbrel,
The sweet sounding lyre with the harp.
3 Blow the trumpet at the new moon,
At the full moon, on our feast day.

Selah 81:7

Superscription 82:0
A Psalm of Asaph.

Selah 82:2

Superscription 83:0
A Song, a Psalm of Asaph.

Selah 83:8

Superscription 84:0
For the choir director; on the Gittith. A Psalm of the sons of Korah.

God's Dwelling Places 84:1-4
2 My soul longed
and even yearned for the courts
of the LORD;
My heart and my flesh sing for joy
to the living God.

Selah 84:4, 8

Superscription 85:0
For the choir director. A Psalm of the sons of Korah.

Selah 85:2

Psalms

Superscription 86:0
A Prayer of David.

Superscription 87:0
A Psalm of the sons of Korah. A Song.

Selah 87:3, 6

Praise to Jerusalem 87:1-7
7 Then those who sing as well as those who
play the flutes *shall say,*
"All my springs *of joy* are in you."

Superscription 88:0
A Song. A Psalm of the sons of Korah. For the choir director; according to *Mahalath Leannoth.* A Maskil of Heman the Ezrahite.

"Mournful lute" is the most likely meaning of *Mahalath Leannoth.*

Selah 88:7, 10

Superscription 89:0
A Maskil of Ethan the Ezrahite.

God's Faithfulness 89:1-4
1 I will sing of the lovingkindness
of the LORD forever;
To all generations I will make known Thy
faithfulness with my mouth.

Selah 89:4, 37, 45, 48

Superscription 90:0
A Prayer of Moses the man of God.

Psalms

Prayer for God's Favor 90:13-17
14 O satisfy us in the morning
with Thy lovingkindness,
That we may sing for joy
and be glad all our days.

Superscription 92:0
A Psalm, a Song for the Sabbath day.

Praise and Thanksgiving 92:1-4
1 It is good to give thanks to the LORD,
And to sing praises
to Thy name,
O Most High;

3 With the ten-stringed lute,
and with the harp;
With resounding music
upon the lyre.
4 For Thou, O LORD, hast made me glad by
what Thou hast done,
I will sing for joy
at the works of Thy hands.

Praise 95:1-5
1 O come, let us sing for joy to the LORD;
Let us shout joyfully
to the rock of our salvation.
2 Let us come before His presence
with thanksgiving;
Let us shout
joyfully to Him
with psalms.

Praise with a New Song 96:1-6
1 Sing to the LORD a new song;
Sing to the LORD, all the earth.

Psalms

2 Sing to the LORD, bless His name;
Proclaim good tidings of His salvation from
day to day.

The Lord Is Coming 96:11-13
12 Let the field exult, and all that is in it.
Then all of the trees of the forest will sing for joy

Superscription 98:0
A Psalm.

Praise 98:1-9
1 O sing to the LORD a new song,
For He has done wonderful things,
His right hand
and His holy arm
have gained the victory for Him.
4 Shout joyfully to the LORD,
all the earth;
Break forth and sing for joy
and sing praises.
5 Sing praises to the LORD
with the lyre;
With the lyre and the sound of melody.
6 With trumpets
and the sound of the horn
Shout joyfully
before the King,
the LORD.

8 Let the rivers clap their hands;
Let the mountains sing together for joy

Superscription 100
A Psalm for Thanksgiving.

Praise to Creator 100:1-3
2 Serve the LORD

Psalms

with gladness;
Come before Him
with joyful singing.

Superscription 101
A Psalm of David.

Profession of Uprightness 101:1-5
1 I will sing
of lovingkindness and justice,
To Thee, O LORD,
I will sing praises.

Superscription 102
A Prayer of the Afflicted, when he is faint, and pours out his complaint before the LORD.

Superscription 103
A *Psalm* of David.

Praise 104:31-35
33 I will sing to the LORD
as long as I live;
I will sing praise to my God
while I have my being.

Praise for God's Wisdom 105:1-7
2 Sing to Him, sing praises to Him;
Speak of all His wonders.

Red Sea Deliverance 106:6-12
12 Then they believed His words;
They sang His praise.

The Lord's Deliverance 107:17-22
22 Let them also offer sacrifices of thanksgiving,
And tell of His works with joyful singing.

Psalms

Superscription 108:0
A Song, a Psalm of David.

Praise and Thanksgiving 108:1-6
1 My heart is steadfast, O God;
I will sing, I will sing praises,
>even with my soul.
2 Awake, harp and lyre;
I will awaken the dawn!
3 I will give thanks to Thee, O LORD,
>among the peoples;
And I will sing praises to Thee
>among the nations.

Superscription 109:0
For the choir director. A Psalm of David.

Superscription 110:0
A Psalm of David.

Deliverance from the Nations 118:10-14
14 The LORD is my strength and song,
And He has become my salvation.

The Lord's Word 119:49-56
54 Thy statutes are my songs
In the house of my pilgrimage.

The next fifteen songs, in the NASB called songs of ascents, can also be titled songs of degrees or, literally, songs of the steps. It is thought that as the pilgrims climbed up the steps of the temple, they would sing these psalms especially, but they could also have simply been sung as the pilgrims traveled to the temple for worship.

Superscriptions 120-134
A Song of Ascents.

Psalms

Praise 135:1-3
3 Praise the LORD,
for the LORD is good;
Sing praises to His name,
for it is lovely.

Music in the Exile 137:1-6
2 Upon the willows in the midst of it
We hung our harps.
3 For there our captors
demanded of us songs,
And our tormentors mirth, *saying*,
"Sing us one of the songs of Zion."
4 How can we sing
the LORD's song
In a foreign land?
5 If I forget you,
O Jerusalem,
May my right hand
forget *her skill*.

Superscription 138:0
A *Psalm* of David.

Temple Worship 138:1-6
1 I will give Thee thanks
with all my heart;
I will sing praises to Thee
before the gods.

5 And they will sing
of the ways of the LORD.
For great is the glory of the LORD.

Superscription 139:0
For the choir director. A *Psalm* of David.

Psalms

Superscription 140:0
For the choir director. A Psalm of David.

Selah 140:3, 5, 8

Superscription 141:0
A Psalm of David.

Superscription 142:0
Maskil of David, when he was in the cave. A Prayer.

Superscription 143:0
A Psalm of David.

Selah 143:6

Superscription 144:0
A *Psalm* of David.

Prayer for Rescue 144:9-11
9 I will sing a new song
to Thee, O God;
Upon a harp of ten strings
I will sing praises
to Thee,

Superscription 145:0
A *Psalm of* Praise, of David.

Praise for Life 146:1-7
2 I will praise the LORD while I live;
I will sing praises to my God
while I have my being.

Praise for the Lord's Works 147:1-11
1 Praise the LORD!
For it is good to sing praises
to our God;

Psalms

> For it is pleasant
> *and* praise is becoming.
>
> **7** Sing to the LORD with thanksgiving;
> Sing praises to our God on the lyre,

Praise 149:1-9
1 Praise the LORD!
Sing to the LORD a new song,
And His praise
in the congregation
of the godly ones.
3 Let them praise His name with dancing;
Let them sing praises to Him
with timbrel and lyre.
5 Let the godly ones exult in glory;
Let them sing for joy on their beds.

Praise 150:1-6
3 Praise Him
with trumpet sound;
Praise Him
with harp and lyre.
4 Praise Him
with timbrel and dancing;
Praise Him
with stringed instruments
and pipe.
5 Praise Him
with loud cymbals;
Praise Him
with resounding cymbals.

The instruments listed here are common ones in the Old Testament. The trumpet is the *shofar* or crooked trumpet; the harp is the *kinnor;* the lyre, sometimes translated *psalter,* is the

Psalms-Proverbs

nehbel; the timbrel or tabret is the *toph;* the stringed instruments are literally strings or *minnim;* pipe is *ugabh;* loud cymbals are *tseltselim.* The only other passage that uses this word for cymbals is 2 Samuel 6:5. The most common Hebrew word for cymbal is *metsiltayim.* All of this is finally concluded with the encompassing verse that everything that has breath should praise the Lord.

This last Psalm is a powerful exhortation to the people of God to praise Him in whatever way possible. It once and for all dispels the notion that we should use only our voices to praise God. He wants to hear our praise in whatever way we can give it. Not only that, this psalm includes every grouping of instruments that we have now: brass, woodwind, string, and percussion.

Those who would argue, as some have, that some instruments, particularly percussion, are not pleasing to God have to disregard many passages that give clear instructions that we are to utilize whatever means possible to praise God. It can, of course, be argued that the Psalms are poetic literature and are not prescriptive in the same way as other Scripture, but there are also many other passages that support the poetic expressions of the Psalms.

Proverbs

Music for the Troubled 25:20
20 *Like* one who takes off a garment on a cold day, *or like* vinegar on soda, Is he who sings songs to a troubled heart.

Music can be downright irritating when one is not in the mood to listen to music. There are some who bounce out of bed in the morning singing, and others need several hours before they can in any way entertain the idea of music in a positive sense. When we encounter those who are diametrically different than we are, we need to be very sensitive. Ecclesiastes 3 very succinctly reminds us that there is a time for everything, but we must discern the appropriateness of every particular action in its particular context. If we don't, even with our music, we will be counterproductive when we so much desire to be a positive ministry.

The Righteous Sing 29:6
6 By transgression an evil man is ensnared,
But the righteous sings and rejoices.

Ecclesiastes

Solomon's Pleasures 2:1-11
8 Also, I collected for myself silver and gold, and the treasure of kings and provinces. I provided for myself male and female singers and the pleasures of men—many concubines.

A Time for Everything 3:1-8
4 A time to weep,
and a time to laugh;
A time to mourn,
and a time to dance.

Rebuke versus Music 7:1-14
5 It is better to listen to the rebuke of a wise man
Than for one to listen to the song of fools.

Old Age 12:1-8
4 and the doors on the street are shut as the sound of the grinding mill is low, and one will arise at the sound of the bird, and all the daughters of song will sing softly.

The Song of Solomon

Note: This whole book is the text of a song.

1:1
1 The Song of Songs, which is Solomon's.

Poets and songsters of all times, move over. However romantic your songs might be, none will match the ardor and passion of this song. To title it the Song of Songs is not arrogant or presumptuous. Although it is often seen by commentators as an allegorical piece describing the love between Christ and the Church, it is probably best to see it as the expression of the pure love between a husband and wife, which includes the physical aspects of love. God intended a man and a woman to love each other with all of their being and intended it to be so from the beginning, when He created Adam and Eve and declared them to be very good. My suggestion is to let this be a love song, as it certainly is, and not try to make it more or less.

Isaiah

Much of Isaiah is poetry, and, as such, might have been sung. Throughout this book Isaiah uses powerful poetry to preach to the Israelites a message of judgment on the one hand, but a message of hope on the other.

A Song for the Beloved 5:1-17
1 Let me sing now
for my well-beloved
A song of my beloved
concerning His vineyard.
My well-beloved
had a vineyard
on a fertile hill.

Isaiah

What follows this introduction is a song that, although it begins sounding like a love song reminiscent of the Song of Songs, soon turns into a song of judgment on the people of Judah who are living contrary to the commands of God. The idea that singing is only for praise and positive thoughts about God and His people is certainly shattered in this song by Isaiah.

Jehovah has built this beautiful vineyard, Israel and Judah, with everything in it needed to bring a bountiful harvest, only to find there is nothing. A song with a delightful beginning soon turns into a song of woe and condemnation.

> **12** And their banquets are *accompanied*
> by lyre and harp,
> by tambourine and flute,
> and by wine;
> But they do not pay attention
> to the deeds of the LORD,
> Nor do they consider
> the work of His hands.

Isaiah lists the lyre *(nebel)*, harp *(kinnor)*, tambourine *(toph)*, and flute *(halil)* as the instruments of choice for entertainment. However, these instruments do not lead the people to heed the deeds of the Lord and the work of His hands.

> *God's Salvation 12:1-6*
> **2** "Behold, God is my salvation,
> I will trust and not be afraid;
> For the LORD God is my strength and song,
> And He has become my salvation."
> **5** Praise the LORD in song,
> for He has done excellent things;
> Let this be known throughout the earth.

The songs sung by the people of God often begin with a personal response to God and His work, but this good news was not

Isaiah

to be selfishly hoarded by the Israelites: this song was to "be known throughout the earth." These "excellent things" were to be trumpeted to all the nations. This is very much in agreement with the tone of the Psalms, which exhort the people to publish the greatness of God to all the nations.

Taunt to Babylon 14:3-21
11 'Your pomp *and* the music of your harps
Have been brought down to Sheol;
Maggots are spread out *as your bed*
beneath you,
And worms are your covering.'

Here is one of the few passages in the Scriptures that suggests a negative judgment on what in the rest of the Bible is seen as a positive activity for the people of God. The verses that follow are often interpreted to refer to Satan and his initial fall from heaven, when he rebelled against God, and to his ultimate destiny. *Nebel,* here translated *harp,* is also often translated *psaltery* in other translations. Normally *kinnor* is translated as *harp.*

Moab 16:6-12
11 Therefore my heart intones
like a harp for Moab,
And my inward feelings
for Kir-hareseth.

This figure of speech is an interesting one in light of contemporary concerns about music being in some way in tune with the body. Those who have tried to show that the body responds to music in negative ways have usually insisted that the incessant rhythm of percussion is the dangerous component of music and ought to be avoided at all costs. Here the writer is expressing an empathy that relates to the music of a harp, which in today's music scene would be considered a very mild and

Isaiah

unobtrusive type of music, certainly not of the sort that would incite to sin or evil of any kind. That music has an influence on the physical element of the human being continues to be a concept that has much intuitive support. But there is still controversy because the empirical evidence is scanty and does not support the claims often made by those who tend to be somewhat contentious on the subject.

This is closely related to the discussion on whether music, apart from the words, can have a negative or positive spiritual influence on a person. Can certain music cause me to sin? Can other music cause me to love God? If the answer to these questions is in the affirmative, we have a tremendous responsibility to then determine which music does which. The safest and most reliable criterion for judging music still seems to be the words. If the music has no words, the judgment needs to be much more tentative. This is closely related to the discussion on whether music, apart from the words, has an effect on the spiritual element of the person.

Cush 18:1-7

3 All you inhabitants of the world
and dwellers on earth,
As soon as a standard
is raised on the mountains,
you will see *it*,
And as soon as the trumpet is blown,
you will hear *it*.

The trumpet in this passage is the *shofar*, which was usually used in war.

Tyre 23:15-18

15 Now it will come about in that day that Tyre will be forgotten for seventy years like the days of one king. At the end of seventy years it will happen to Tyre as *in* the song of the harlot:

Isaiah

> **16** Take your harp,
> walk about the city,
> O forgotten harlot;
> Pluck the strings skillfully,
> sing many songs,
> That you may be remembered.

Harp in this verse is translated from *kinnor.* To "Pluck the strings skillfully" comes from *naggen,* possibly an instrument similar to the harp because it also requires plucking. The prophecy against Tyre is not a pleasant one. It begins with "Wail, O ships of Tarshish," a fearful harbinger of the judgment to come. It is in this context of the prophecy against Tyre that Isaiah says Tyre will be forgotten for seventy years and quotes the harlot's song of verse 16.

The song paints the picture of the forlorn harlot who when young was beautiful and desired by many but now is old and haggard and has been replaced by others. This is Tyre. But then when the song ends, a seemingly contradictory explanation indicates that Tyre will go back to harlotry but the gains will be set apart to the Lord to become food and attire for the those who dwell in God's presence. The Lord's purposes certainly are often not easily understood.

> *The LORD's Judgment 24:7-23*
> **8** The gaiety of tambourines ceases,
> The noise of revelers stops,
> The gaiety of the harp ceases.
> **9** They do not drink wine with song;
> Strong drink is bitter to those who drink it.
>
> **16** From the ends of the earth
> we hear songs,
> "Glory to the Righteous One,"
> But I say, "Woe to me!
> Woe to me!

Isaiah

> Alas for me!
> The treacherous
> deal treacherously,
> And the treacherous
> deal very treacherously."

The tambourines *(toph)* and the harp *(kinnor)* cease. The revelers stop. Intense grief and music simply do not coexist easily. The prophecy that the earth will be devastated is followed by a commentary in song. Wine and music, which for the partying kind usually join to provide a powerful combination of sensory pleasures, are now both nauseous to the inhabitants of this country.

Song in Judah 26:1-6
1 In that day this song will be sung in the land of Judah:
> "We have a strong city;
> He sets up walls and ramparts for security.

Song of Victory 27:1-6
2 In that day,
> "A vineyard of wine,
> sing of it!

Song of Victory 27:12, 13
13 It will come about also in that day that a great trumpet will be blown; and those who were perishing in the land of Assyria and who were scattered in the land of Egypt will come and worship the LORD in the holy mountain at Jerusalem.

The trumpet here is the *shofar* or crooked trumpet.

The LORD's Anger against the Nations 30:27-33
29 You will have songs
> as in the night
> when you keep the festival;
> And gladness of heart as when one marches
> to *the sound of* the flute,

Isaiah

> To go to the mountain of the LORD,
> to the Rock of Israel.
> **32** And every blow of the rod of punishment,
> Which the LORD will lay on him,
> Will be *with the music
> of* tambourines and lyres;
> And in battles, brandishing weapons,
> He will fight them.

The flute *(halil)*, the tambourine *(toph)*, and the *lyres (kinnor)* are the instruments listed here as the ones God will use to accompany the judgment and punishment of the king of Assyria.

> *Prayer and Thanksgiving 38:10-20*
> **20** "The LORD will surely save me;
> So we will play my songs on stringed instruments
> All *the* days of our life at the house of the LORD."

> *Exhortation to Praise 42:10-13*
> **10** Sing to the LORD a new song,
> *Sing* His praise from the end of the earth!
> You who go down to the sea,
> and all that is in it.
> You islands and those who dwell on them.
> **11** Let the wilderness and its cities
> lift up *their voices,*
> The settlements where Kedar inhabits.
> Let the inhabitants of Sela sing aloud,
> Let them shout for joy from the
> tops of the mountains.

> *Comfort by the Lord 51:1-3*
> **3** Indeed, the LORD will comfort Zion;
> He will comfort all her waste places.
> And her wilderness He will make like Eden,
> And her desert like the garden of the LORD;
> Joy and gladness will be found in her,

Isaiah-Jeremiah

Thanksgiving and sound of a melody.

A Call to Righteousness 58:1
1 "Cry loudly, do not hold back;
Raise your voice like a trumpet,
And declare to My people their transgression,
And to the house of Jacob their sins.

Jeremiah

Note: Much of Jeremiah is poetry, and as such might have been sung.

Call to Repentance 4:5-8
5 Declare in Judah
and proclaim in Jerusalem, and say,
"Blow the trumpet in the land;
Cry aloud and say,
'Assemble yourselves, and let us go
Into the fortified cities.'

Soul Anguish 4:19-22
19 My soul, my soul!
I am in anguish!
Oh, my heart!
My heart is pounding in me;
I cannot be silent,
Because you have heard,
O my soul,
The sound of the trumpet,
The alarm of war.

21 How long must I see the standard,
And hear the sound of the trumpet?

Warning of God's Judgment 6:1-8
1 "Flee for safety, O sons of Benjamin,

Jeremiah

From the midst of Jerusalem!
Now blow a trumpet in Tekoa,
And raise a signal over Beth-haccerem;
For evil looks down from the north,
And a great destruction.

Warning of God's Judgment 6:16-21
17 "And I set watchmen over you, *saying*,
'Listen to the sound of the trumpet!'
But they said, 'We will not listen.'

False Prophecy 20:7-13
13 Sing to the LORD, praise the LORD!
For He has delivered
the soul of the needy one
From the hand of evildoers.

Deliverance by the Lord 31:1-9
4 "Again I will build you, and you shall be
rebuilt, O virgin of Israel!
Again you shall take up your tambourines,
And go forth to the dances of
the merry-makers.
7 For thus says the LORD,
"Sing aloud with gladness for Jacob,
And shout among the chiefs of the nations;
Proclaim, give praise, and say,
'O LORD, save Thy people,
The remnant of Israel.'

Prophecy to the Nations 31:10-14
13 "Then the virgin
shall rejoice in the dance,
And the young men
and the old, together,
For I will turn their mourning into joy,
And will comfort them,

Jeremiah

and give them joy
for their sorrow.

Promises to Israel 42:7-17

14 saying, "No, but we will go to the land of Egypt, where we shall not see war or hear the sound of a trumpet or hunger for bread, and we will stay there";

Sorrow for Moab 48:36-44

36 "Therefore My heart wails for Moab like flutes; My heart also wails like flutes for the men of Kir-heres. Therefore they have lost the abundance it produced.

This passage indicates the depth of sorrow that probably only God is capable of. *Hamah,* the word translated *wails,* suggests a murmur or growl coming from God's most inner being.

Sorrow for Ammon 49:1-6

2 "Therefore behold,
the days are coming," declares the Lord,
"That I shall cause a trumpet blast of war to be heard
Against Rabbah of the sons of Ammon;
And it will become a desolate heap,
And her towns will be set on fire.
Then Israel will take possession of his possessors,"
Says the Lord.

Summons to the Nations 51:27-32

27 Lift up a signal in the land,
Blow a trumpet among the nations!
Consecrate the nations against her,
Summon against her the kingdoms of Ararat,
Minni and Ashkenaz;
Appoint a marshal against her,
Bring up the horses like bristly locusts.

Lamentations

Mockery by the People 3:1-18
14 I have become a laughingstock to all my people,
Their *mocking* song all the day.

Mockery by the People 3:59-63
63 Look on their sitting and their rising,
I am their mocking song.

This book is a true lament. In this chapter (the middle of the book), it turns into stark, staccato couplets bemoaning the state of the people of Israel. There is little in this book that gives relief from the desolate scene of God having allowed the people to go their own way and the consequences that have followed. The writer feels very keenly that he has become the subject of mockery and reiterates this several times in this section.

Results of Judgment 5:1-18
14 Elders are gone from the gate,
Young men from their music.
15 The joy of our hearts has ceased;
Our dancing has been turned into mourning.

Ezekiel

Prophecy 7:14-22
14 'They have blown the trumpet and made everything ready, but no one is going to the battle; for My wrath is against all their multitude.

Prophecy about Tyre 26:7-14
13 "So I will silence the sound of your songs, and the sound of your harps will be heard no more.

Ezekiel

The Watchman's Responsibility 33:1-6

3 and he sees the sword coming upon the land, and he blows on the trumpet and warns the people,

4 then he who hears the sound of the trumpet and does not take warning, and a sword comes and takes him away, his blood will be on his *own* head.

5 'He heard the sound of the trumpet, but did not take warning; his blood will be on himself. But had he taken warning, he would have delivered his life.

6 'But if the watchman sees the sword coming and does not blow the trumpet, and the people are not warned, and a sword comes and takes a person from them, he is taken away in his iniquity; but his blood I will require from the watchman's hand.'

The *shofar* or crooked trumpet continues to be the instrument that is employed to rouse people, either to action in a battle situation or, in this case, to warn people that there is impending danger, possibly also war. This passage has been used to exhort believers to be more diligent in warning others of the coming judgment and encouraging them to turn to God before the sword of judgment falls. This word from the prophet is still relevant today because there is a final judgment coming.

Hypocrisy 33:30-33

32 "And behold, you are to them like a sensual song by one who has a beautiful voice and plays well on an instrument; for they hear your words, but they do not practice them.

The recurring theme in these verses is the voice that speaks words but the words do not have the impact that they should. There is an outward acquiescence, but inwardly there is a disregard for the truth expressed by the prophet. On the one hand, the people do the lustful things that their mouths express, and on the other hand, they hear the words of the Lord but do not practice them. The figure of speech here employed likens this all to a sensual song sung by a beautiful voice and accompanied by a skillfully played instrument.

Picture a love song suggesting the pleasures of the body, a velvet, low, crooning voice with an accompaniment that is skillfully nuanced to tease with an invitation to respond but also to keep you at a distance and never allow satisfaction. So it is with words that are empty. They simply lead on, implying that gratification is coming. But it never does because it is all based on a deception that cannot satisfy.

Temple Descriptions 40:44-47

44 And from the outside to the inner gate were chambers for the singers in the inner court, *one of* which was at the side of the north gate, with its front toward the south, and one at the side of the east gate facing toward the north.

Daniel

Nebuchadnezzar's Gold Image 3:1-18

5 that at the moment you hear the sound of the horn, flute, lyre, trigon, psaltery, bagpipe, and all kinds of music, you are to fall down and worship the golden image that Nebuchadnezzar the king has set up.

7 Therefore at that time, when all the peoples heard the sound of the horn, flute, lyre, trigon, psaltery, bagpipe, and all kinds of music, all the peoples, nations and *men of every* language fell down *and* worshiped the golden image that Nebuchadnezzar the king had set up.

10 "You yourself, O king, have made a decree that every man who hears the sound of the horn, flute, lyre, trigon, psaltery, and bagpipe, and all kinds of music, is to fall down and worship the golden image.

15 "Now if you are ready, at the moment you hear the sound

Daniel

of the horn, flute, lyre, trigon, psaltery, and bagpipe, and all kinds of music, to fall down and worship the image that I have made, *very well*. But if you will not worship, you will immediately be cast into the midst of a furnace of blazing fire; and what god is there who can deliver you out of my hands?"

This is one of the classic passages in Daniel where these three men, Shadrach, Meshach, and Abed-nego (we don't know where Daniel was during this incident), who had been brought from the land of Israel to serve the pagan king, stand straight and tall with conviction and refuse to obey a command of a king. This meant death. To them that made no difference. The question that Nebuchadnezzar asks at the end of verse 15 is meant to be rhetorical, but it is answered very clearly when the men do not burn in the furnace. To bend the knee to the king in this case was without doubt worshipping the king and denying God. To the Israelites the decision was clear.

In this passage the music served as the signal to the bureaucrats of Babylon that they were to fall down and worship the image commissioned by the king. One might think that falling down would have been sufficient, but there was some aspect to the event that required worship after they were kneeling (or possibly prostrating). Whether this meant that words were to be spoken or whether further actions were required we do not know. Whatever the case, to the king this was very serious and abstaining was not tolerated.

In the worship of the people of God, the relationship between music and worship has always been strong. Obviously it was the same in this pagan culture. A huge orchestra, a huge statue, the elite of the country, and the command of the king were the ingredients that combined to make this an event that would please the gods of the nation but more so the ego of King Nebuchadnezzar.

This list of instruments is probably the longest in the Scriptures. Four times these instruments are listed as the drama unfolds. It was as impressive then as it is now. The Babylonians obviously had a very highly developed music culture. The list, with italic terms in Aramaic, is as follows:

horn *(qeren)*,
flute *(mashroqiytha)* found only in Daniel,
lyre *(qitharos)*,
trigon *(sabbeka)*,
psaltery *(pesantrin)*,
bagpipe *(sumponeyah)*,
and all kinds of music *(zemar)*.

How many there were of each, we do not know. One could presume that there were many, especially since each time it is also mentioned that it was these particular instruments and also all kinds of music.

Hosea

Israel's Restoration 2:14-20
15 "Then I will give her her vineyards from there,
And the valley of Achor
as a door of hope.
And she will sing there
as in the days of her youth,
As in the day when she came up
from the land of Egypt.

In this highly figurative book, the land of Israel is described as a harlot because of her continuing, deliberate unfaithfulness. Hosea has been told by God to take a harlot as a wife to symbolize God's wooing of the nation to return to Him and His readiness to forgive and renew the broken relationship.

One of the activities of the former days was singing. When Israel comes back to the Lord she will sing as she did in her youth. As it was then, singing often accompanies renewal among God's people. To sing the Lord's songs is not easy when the relationship is broken.

Judgment against Israel 5:8-15
8 Blow the horn in Gibeah,
The trumpet in Ramah.
Sound an alarm at Beth-aven:
"Behind you, Benjamin!"

The instruments here are the *shofar*, the crooked trumpet, and the *chatsotsrah*, the straight trumpet.

Israel's Transgression 8:1-7
1 *Put* the trumpet to your lips!
Like an eagle *the enemy comes*
against the house of the LORD,
Because they have transgressed My covenant,
And rebelled against My law.

The trumpet is the *shofar.*

Joel

Prophecy 2:1-17
1 Blow a trumpet in Zion,
And sound an alarm on My holy mountain!
Let all the inhabitants of the land tremble,
For the day of the LORD is coming;
Surely it is near,

15 Blow a trumpet in Zion,
Consecrate a fast, proclaim a solemn assembly,

Both of these verses refer to the *shofar,* the crooked trumpet often used to announce an event or to rally the people to war or some other action.

Amos

Judgment on Moab 2:1-3
2 "So I will send fire upon Moab,
And it will consume the citadels of Kerioth;
And Moab will die amid tumult,
With war cries and the sound of a trumpet.

The instrument in this passage is the *shofar.*

Witness against Israel 3:2-8
6 If a trumpet is blown in a city
will not the people tremble?
If a calamity occurs in a city
has not the LORD done it?

The instrument again is the *shofar.*

Offerings Rejected by God 5:21-24
23 "Take away from Me
the noise of your songs;
I will not even listen
to the sound of your harps.

This is one of the sharpest denunciations by this prophet. Amos has been appealing to the Israelites to turn back to God and has pointed out to them the folly of their ways. But at this juncture of his exhortation he focuses, in quite a sudden way, on the actions that would normally please God and lambasts them about their festivals, assemblies, offerings, and music. These worship events seem to be the ultimate in hypocrisy. The noise

Amos

of their songs *(shir)* and the sound of their harps *(nebel)* cannot override the condition of their hearts, which are far from God.

Lifestyle Rejected by God 6:4-7
5 Who improvise
to the sound of the harp,
And like David
have composed songs for themselves,

While the previous passage pointed out the hypocrisy of trying to worship when the heart was not right, this passage points to Israel's rich and selfish lifestyle as another hindrance in relating to God. A part of their musical activity was to improvise to the sound of the harp. David, the "sweet psalmist of Israel," did not write songs only for his own pleasure, as these people did, but wrote them as offerings of praise to God. For these who felt so at ease in Zion, all of the musical activity was simply for their own pleasure. God saw nothing redeeming in their music making.

Judgment on Israel 8:1-10
3 "The songs of the palace will turn to wailing in that day," declares the Lord God. "Many *will be* the corpses; in every place they will cast them forth in silence."

10 "Then I shall turn your festivals into mourning
And all your songs into lamentation;
And I will bring sackcloth on everyone's loins
And baldness on every head.
And I will make it like *a time of* mourning
for an only son,
And the end of it will be like a bitter day.

God is reacting to the injustice of the wealthy and the powerful who have been cheating the poor and needy. There will be wailing and lamentations as the judgment comes. The songs of the palace and the music mentioned earlier in the book, which had been sources of pleasure, will turn to mourning. Almost inevitably when there is mourning, music ceases.

Obadiah

There are no references to music in the Book of Obadiah.

Jonah

There are no references to music in the Book of Jonah.

Micah

There are no references to music in the Book of Micah.

Nahum

There are no references to music in the Book of Nahum.

Habakkuk

Note: All of Habakkuk is the text of a song. It was likely intended to be sung to the accompaniment of musical instruments. All of it is vigorous verse describing the ferocity of the Chaldeans.

Judgment for Greed 2:6-8
6 "Will not all of these take up a taunt-song
against him,
Even mockery *and* insinuations against him,
And say, 'Woe to him who increases what is not his—
For how long—
And makes himself rich with loans?'

Habakkuk

Shigionoth 3:1
1 A prayer of Habakkuk the prophet, according to Shigionoth.

Shigionoth is translated variously as an ode or song, a wandering, plaintive song, or, as in the NASB, a highly emotional poetic form.

Selah 3:3, 9, 13

Resolution to Rejoice 3:16-19
19 The Lord GOD is my strength,
And He has made my feet like hinds' *feet,*
And makes me walk on my high places.

For the choir director, on my stringed instruments.

The most remarkable part of this short, poetic, prophetic book is the last few verses. After the prophet has held forth so eloquently about the Chaldeans and their cruelties, he culminates it all with a striking sextuplet,

Though the fig tree should not blossom,
And there be no fruit on the vines,
Though the yield of the olive should fail,
And the fields produce no food,
Though the flocks should be cut off from the fold,
And there be no cattle in the stalls,

Which is followed by that powerful commitment,

Yet I will exult in the LORD,
I will rejoice in the God of my salvation.

All of this, and more of course, is offered to the Lord to the accompaniment of stringed instruments *(negonith).*

Zephaniah

The Day of the Lord 1:14-18
16 A day of trumpet and battle cry,
Against the fortified cities
And the high corner towers.

The trumpet *(shofar)* is again referred to as an instrument of war.

Judgment against the Nations 2:12-15
14 And flocks will lie down in her midst,
All beasts which range in herds;
Both the pelican and the hedgehog
Will lodge in the tops of her pillars;
Birds will sing in the window,
Desolation *will be* on the threshold;
For He has laid bare the cedar work.

The sophisticated city of Nineveh will become desolate and will be inhabited by the wild beasts. One of those will be the birds singing in the window.

Haggai

There are no references to music in the Book of Haggai.

Zechariah

The Lord's Presence Promised 2:6-13
10 "Sing for joy and be glad,
O daughter of Zion;
for behold I am coming
and I will dwell in your midst,"
declares the Lord.

The exhortation to sing because the Lord is coming to live in the midst of them is a good one and well understood by the Israelites. The verse that follows, however, is one that they found more difficult to understand and accept. God had continually told the Jews that they were His chosen people. In this verse God's larger purpose is very clear. Many nations, says the prophet, will join themselves to the Lord and will become His people.

It was never God's intention to limit salvation to one nation. This becomes very evident in the New Testament when Jesus leaves and Paul, especially, begins preaching to the Gentiles. This is a continuation of the theme of redemption of the whole world that flows throughout the Bible.

The LORD's Help in Conquest 9:11-17
14 Then the LORD
will appear over them,
And His arrow
will go forth like lightning;
And the Lord GOD
will blow the trumpet,
And will march in the storm winds
of the south.

Once again the *shofar* is depicted as the instrument for announcement or war.

Malachi

There are no references to music in the Book of Malachi.

NEW TESTAMENT

There is a remarkable absence of references to music in the New Testament. While in the Old Testament there are scenes of celebration, worship, praise, victory, entertainment, therapy, and a variety of other occasions, in the New Testament this social and religious phenomenon is quite conspicuously absent. Why this difference?

Matthew

Giving of Alms 6:1-4

2 "When therefore you give alms, do not sound a trumpet before you, as the hypocrites do in the synagogues and in the streets, that they may be honored by men. Truly I say to you, they have their reward in full.

Although less dramatic than some of the announcements in the Old Testament, the trumpet is still utilized to get the attention of people. This use for the instrument is certainly less than laudable, but it is nevertheless effective. The original language in the New Testament is Greek, and the original word for trumpet is *salpigx*.

Girl Raised from the Dead 9:18-26

23 And when Jesus came into the official's house, and saw the flute-players, and the crowd in noisy disorder,

The flute-players *(auletas)* were part of the mourning party. Apparently the flutes would blend in to the sound of mourners wailing. The accounts of mourning do not normally include music, at least not music that is joyful or uplifting. The music of the flutes is more likely to have been doleful dirges that supported the mourning scene. The scene Jesus encountered certainly did not seem to be one where an orderly musical presentation would have been accepted.

Jesus Speaking of John the Baptist 11:7-19

17 and say, 'We played the flute for you, and you did not dance; we sang a dirge, and you did not mourn.'

Because John was not what the Jewish leaders expected, they did not respond to the music. They were determined to provide the music for the people, and if it wasn't provided by them, they wouldn't dance or mourn. The music was meant to

Matthew

prompt them to respond appropriately, but they wouldn't.

Herod's Daughter 14:1-12
6 But when Herod's birthday came, the daughter of Herodias danced before *them* and pleased Herod.

The dance in this case was the catalyst to John's beheading. His young niece's dance pleased Herod to the extent that he promised her up to half his kingdom. The evil mother used this sensual event to her advantage to get rid of a severe irritant, John the Baptist, who had objected to her relationship to Herod. Though the dance was pleasurable to Herod, it later brought him much anguish when he realized he would have to grant the request to keep his honor among his peers.

End-Time Prophecy 24:29-31
31 "And He will send forth His angels with a great trumpet and they will gather together His elect from the four winds, from one end of the sky to the other.

The end of time, Jesus' coming, is consistently described as an event of power and triumph. The trumpet *(salpigx)* is usually the instrument indicated to be the one that will announce this culmination of history as we know it. Angels playing trumpets conjure up a sound that is far from the sound we often hear from brass players, especially those who are at the very beginning of their playing experience.

Brass instruments in perfect harmony produce a wonderful sound and have traditionally, in our culture, been used to announce the approach of royalty. On the occasion foretold here, the King of Kings will be announced by a sound from a multitude of angels that I think is beyond imagination. It is quite conceivable that the trumpets are only the symbol of all that will be played on that day. Why not a brass choir consisting of multitudes of angels and instruments?

Matthew-Luke

Last Supper 26:26-30
30 And after singing a hymn, they went out to the Mount of Olives.

Mark

Herodias' Daughter 6:14-29
22 and when the daughter of Herodias herself came in and danced, she pleased Herod and his dinner guests; and the king said to the girl, "Ask me for whatever you want and I will give it to you."

Last Supper 14:22-26
26 And after singing a hymn, they went out to the Mount of Olives.

Luke

Jesus Speaking of John the Baptist 7:24-35
32 "They are like children who sit in the market place and call to one another; and they say,
> 'We played the flute for you,
> and you did not dance;
> we sang a dirge,
> and you did not weep.'

The Prodigal Son 15:11-32
25 "Now his older son was in the field, and when he came and approached the house, he heard music and dancing.

The response of the father and the household was as natural as could be expected. Feasts in those days were always events of much music and food. The music *(sumphonia)* could be heard from a distance and was not likely just a few instruments.

Luke-Acts

A sizable orchestra would have befit an event commemorating the coming to life of one who had been dead and was now alive, lost and now found.

Jesus, David's Son 20:41-44
42 "For David himself says in the book of Psalms,
'The LORD said to my Lord,
"Sit at My right hand,

Jesus Expounds the Scriptures 24:44-49
44 Now He said to them, "These are My words which I spoke to you while I was still with you, that all things which are written about Me in the Law of Moses and the Prophets and the Psalms must be fulfilled."

Jesus does not appeal only to the Law and the Prophets when He refers to the Old Testament, but also to the Psalms, the music of the Scriptures.

John

There are no references to music in the Gospel of John.

Acts

Peter Speaks 1:15-26
20 "For it is written in the book of Psalms,
'Let his homestead
be made desolate,
And let no man dwell in it';
and, 'His office
let another man take.'

Acts-Romans

Paul Preaches 13:16-41

33 that God has fulfilled this *promise* to our children in that He raised up Jesus, as it is also written in the second Psalm, 'Thou art My Son; today I have begotten Thee.'

35 "Therefore He also says in another *Psalm,* 'Thou wilt not allow Thy Holy One to undergo decay.'

Following the example of Jesus, Peter and Paul refer to the Psalms to provide evidence of being the fulfillment of prophecy.

Paul and Silas in Prison 16:19-40

25 But about midnight Paul and Silas were praying and singing hymns of praise to God, and the prisoners were listening to them;

No one can stop you from singing if you want to sing. Paul and Silas had all the reason in the world to be "down in the mouth," but after being beaten and fastened into stocks, they prayed and sang. Was the earthquake a result of their singing? God certainly heard them and did a miracle by releasing them and giving salvation to the jailer and his family.

Romans

Old Testament Quotes 15:7-13

9 and for the Gentiles to glorify God for His mercy; as it is written,

> "Therefore I will give praise to Thee
> among the Gentiles,
> And I will sing to Thy name."

This verse is the beginning of a series of quotes from the Psalms supporting the idea, a difficult one for the Jews, that the Gentiles would also be saved.

1 Corinthians

Love 13:1-3

1 If I speak with the tongues of men and of angels, but do not have love, I have become a noisy gong or a clanging cymbal.

The noisy gong *(chalkos echeo)* refers to sound on the one hand and to brass on the other hand. This could mean that the instrument was a wind instrument, but it could also be a brass gong. Some translations opt for the trumpet; this one chose the gong.

Spiritual Gifts 14:1-33

7 Yet *even* lifeless things, either flute or harp, in producing a sound, if they do not produce a distinction in the tones, how will it be known what is played on the flute or on the harp?
8 For if the bugle produces an indistinct sound, who will prepare himself for battle?

15 What is *the outcome* then? I shall pray with the spirit and I shall pray with the mind also; I shall sing with the spirit and I shall sing with the mind also.

26 What is *the outcome* then, brethren? When you assemble, each one has a psalm, has a teaching, has a revelation, has a tongue, has an interpretation. Let all things be done for edification.

Paul is addressing the serious problem of confusion and disorder in the Corinthian church. To make his point that an unclear or mixed message is counterproductive, he resorts to an example from music. The flute *(aulos)* and the harp *(kithara)* are the first two instruments noted, followed by the bugle *(salpigx)*. A melody, to be recognized, requires that the tones be distinct from each other; a message of words requires intelligibility if the message is to be understood. In preaching the gospel this is particularly crucial.

The point Paul wants to make is that in speaking in tongues the spirit is active and engaged but the mind isn't (v. 14). Paul advocates praying and singing with both the mind and the spirit so that both the individual speaking and singing as well as the corporate body will be edified. To insist on speaking in tongues is therefore a selfish indulgence unless there is a systematic program of interpretation so that all can benefit.

Jesus' Second Coming 15:50-58

52 in a moment, in the twinkling of an eye, at the last trumpet; for the trumpet will sound, and the dead will be raised imperishable, and we shall be changed.

Again, the trumpet is the instrument indicated as the one we will hear when Jesus comes.

2 Corinthians

There are no references to music in 2 Corinthians.

Galatians

There are no references to music in Galatians.

Ephesians

Filling of the Spirit 5:15-21

19 speaking to one another in psalms and hymns and spiritual songs, singing and making melody with your heart to the Lord;

This is one of the two classic passages on music in the New

Ephesians

Testament. Invariably when writers on Christian music discuss the music of the New Testament they will refer to this verse. The context of this verse is one where Paul warns against foolishness, wasting time, and drunkenness, and instructs that we are to "be filled with the Spirit." This is the pivotal phrase, after which Paul gives positive instructions that include speaking to one another, giving thanks, and being subject to one another. This could be seen as an arch form with "being filled with the Spirit "as the overarching thought that ties all of this together, showing what a difference the filling of the Spirit makes.

Being filled with the Spirit

Foolishness	Being subject to others
Wasting time	Giving thanks
Drunkenness	Speaking to one another

Drunkenness is a condition that will likely lead to a loss of self-control; Paul wants us to be controlled by the Spirit rather than by wine. While drunkenness might lead to singing and ribaldry, this is not the kind of singing that the Holy Spirit will bring. The Holy Spirit will produce psalms *(psalmos)*, hymns *(humnos)*, and spiritual songs (*ode pneumatikos*) in the believer. Although we recognize that Paul intended a distinction between these types of songs, we do not know, apart from speculation, what the exact distinctions were. To force on these terms our own contemporary distinctions is to force our present language and template on genres that we cannot clearly differentiate.

The music inspired by the Holy Spirit goes in two directions: horizontally to one another in fellowship and vertically by a melody in the heart to the Lord. In all of our worship and fellowship we need to keep these two directions in mind. To think one can fellowship with the Lord when one can't fellowship with the brothers and sisters or to think one can have meaningful fellowship with believers when things are not right between one and the Lord is to have a wrong conception of the totality of the relational life of a growing, maturing Christian. A part of this relationship is expressed in music.

Philippians

There are no references to music in Philippians.

Colossians

Holy Living 3:12-17

16 Let the word of Christ richly dwell within you, with all wisdom teaching and admonishing one another with psalms *and* hymns *and* spiritual songs, singing with thankfulness in your hearts to God.

This is the second of the two classic passages on music in the New Testament. Paul here expands the idea of fellowship through music by adding that we are to teach and exhort with psalms, hymns, and spiritual songs with thanksgiving. The heart is again the organ that transmits this to God. The consistent emphasis in both of these passages is that the ministry of music is bidirectional: to one another and to God.

1 Thessalonians

Jesus' Second Coming 4:1-18

16 For the Lord Himself will descend from heaven with a

shout, with the voice of *the* archangel, and with the trumpet of God; and the dead in Christ shall rise first.

We will rise to the sound of music! Brass is definitely the loudest of the instrument families, other than possibly percussion. I expect not just loud blasts but beautiful melody and harmony in absolute perfect pitch. I think it will be the voice of the archangel that will cause us to rise, not the trumpet. But as we rise, we will be greeted by this most wonderful brass choir of angels, who have either rehearsed all of these years or are so good that they have never needed to rehearse.

2 Thessalonians

There are no references to music in Second Thessalonians.

1-2 Timothy

There are no references to music in Paul's Letters to Timothy.

Titus

There are no references to music in Titus.

Philemon

There are no references to music in Philemon.

Hebrews

Jesus Fellowships with the Brethren 2:5-18

12 saying,
  "I will proclaim Thy name to My brethren,

In the midst of the congregation I will
sing Thy praise."

This verse is a quotation from Psalm 22:22.

Giving of the Commandments 12:18-29
19 and to the blast of a trumpet and the sound of words which *sound was such that* those who heard begged that no further word should be spoken to them.

This is a reference to Exodus 20:18, which records this exact event and the peoples' response to the Lord's revelation to them. The sensory assault of the thunder, lightning, trumpet, cloud, and smoke was so intense that the people begged Moses to speak himself rather than have God speak to them directly.

James

Healing for the Sick 5:13-18
13 Is anyone among you suffering? Let him pray. Is anyone cheerful? Let him sing praises.

Although the passage is focused on prayer, and especially on praying for the sick, there is a brief allusion to singing. If someone is merry he is to sing. The three questions relate to three situations:

1. suffering behooves prayer
2. cheerfulness begets singing
3. sickness requires the elders

The model prescribed here underlines several concepts that are important in the situation where someone is sick. The church is to be involved. The faith of the elders will make the difference. Confession might be necessary—not just by the one who is sick, but also by others, maybe even the elders. Forgiveness will be given. Sickness will be healed.

1-2 Peter

There are no references to music in Peter's Letters.

1-3 John

There are no references to music in John's Letters.

Jude

There are no references to music in Jude.

Revelation

The Voice of the Lord 1:9-20
10 I was in the Spirit on the Lord's day, and I heard behind me a loud voice like *the sound* of a trumpet,

The references to music in the Revelation are of several different types. In this one and the next one, the sound of a voice is said to be like the sound of a trumpet *(salpingos)*; it is not an actual trumpet. The voice in these cases is the voice of the Lord who is the King and gives instruction about recording what John has seen. Since he is royalty of royalty, it is suitable that the instrument of royalty would be the comparison.

The Throne in Heaven 4:1-11
1 After these things I looked, and behold, a door *standing*

Revelation

open in heaven, and the first voice which I had heard, like *the sound* of a trumpet speaking with me, said, "Come up here, and I will show you what must take place after these things."

The verses following also indicate very clearly that it is the Lord who is speaking and whose voice sounds like a trumpet.

The Lamb and the Scroll 5:1-14

8 And when He had taken the book, the four living creatures and the twenty-four elders fell down before the Lamb, having each one a harp, and golden bowls full of incense, which are the prayers of the saints.
9 And they *sang a new song, saying,
"Worthy art Thou
to take the book,
and to break its seals;
for Thou wast slain,
and didst purchase for God
with Thy blood
Men from every tribe
and tongue and people and nation.

The scene of worship and celebration continues in this passage as we're presented with the twenty-four elders with their harps *(kithara)* and incense. Presumably they accompany the song they sing to the Lamb. It is not often that one hears a harp choir. In our day we don't often hear a guitar choir, even though it is probably the most popular instrument of our generation. The song is a missionary song that summarizes the work of the evangelists who have gone to all tribes, tongues, peoples and nations to tell them of the work of the Lamb.

The Seven Trumpets 8:2-13

2 And I saw the seven angels who stand before God; and seven trumpets were given to them.

Revelation

6 And the seven angels who had the seven trumpets prepared themselves to sound them.

7 And the first sounded, and there came hail and fire, mixed with blood, and they were thrown to the earth; and a third of the earth was burned up, and a third of the trees were burned up, and all the green grass was burned up.

8 And the second angel sounded, and *something* like a great mountain burning with fire was thrown into the sea; and a third of the sea became blood;

10 And the third angel sounded, and a great star fell from heaven, burning like a torch, and it fell on a third of the rivers and on the springs of waters;

12 And the fourth angel sounded, and a third of the sun and a third of the moon and a third of the stars were smitten, so that a third of them might be darkened and the day might not shine for a third of it, and the night in the same way.

13 And I looked, and I heard an eagle flying in midheaven, saying with a loud voice, "Woe, woe, woe, to those who dwell on the earth, because of the remaining blasts of the trumpet of the three angels who are about to sound!"

The Seven Trumpets 9:1-21

1 And the fifth angel sounded, and I saw a star from heaven which had fallen to the earth; and the key of the bottomless pit was given to him.

13 And the sixth angel sounded, and I heard a voice from the four horns of the golden altar which is before God,

14 one saying to the sixth angel who had the trumpet, "Release the four angels who are bound at the great river Euphrates."

The Seven Trumpets 10:1-11

7 but in the days of the voice of the seventh angel, when he is about to sound, then the mystery of God is finished, as He preached to His servants the prophets.

Revelation

The Seven Trumpets 11:1-15

15 And the seventh angel sounded; and there arose loud voices in heaven, saying,

"The kingdom of the world has become *the kingdom* of our Lord, and of His Christ; and He will reign forever and ever."

The twenty-four elders were each carrying a harp, but these angels were given trumpets that turned out to be trumpets heralding judgment. In each case, when the trumpet was sounded a catastrophe occurred on the earth. The sound of trumpets at the end of time will not only announce the wonder of Jesus' return to His children, but will also announce the coming of judgment to His enemies. The same instrument will on the one hand be the welcome sound of deliverance to some, and on the other hand be the awful sound of destruction to others.

The 144,000 14:1-5

2 And I heard a voice from heaven, like the sound of many waters and like the sound of loud thunder, and the voice which I heard *was* like *the sound* of harpists playing on their harps.
3 And they *sang a new song before the throne and before the four living creatures and the elders; and no one could learn the song except the one hundred and forty-four thousand who had been purchased from the earth.

For a voice to sound like the sound of many harpists is a bit more of a stretch than to say it sounds like a trumpet, but that is how the voice of the Lord is described here. It is sweet and tinkling rather than loud and blasting.

Seven Angels and Seven Plagues 15:1-4

2 And I saw, as it were, a sea of glass mixed with fire, and those who had come off victorious from the beast and from

Revelation

his image and from the number of his name, standing on the sea of glass, holding harps of God.

3 And they *sang the song of Moses the bond-servant of God and the song of the Lamb, saying, "Great and marvelous are Thy works, O Lord God, the Almighty; Righteous and true are Thy ways, Thou King of the nations.

Although this is called the song of Moses, it is not a quotation from one of Moses' songs in the Old Testament. The combining of Jesus and Moses as the composers or owners of this song indicates the importance of Moses in the salvation story in the Scriptures. The whole story of the exodus is the story of the Israelites' salvation from the Egyptians who had enslaved them for four hundred years. Moses was the leader in this, without whom this forty-year delivery might not have been possible. And of course, salvation for humanity would not have been possible without Jesus.

Babylon Defeated 18:21-24

22 "And the sound of harpists and musicians and flute-players and trumpeters will not be heard in you any longer; and no craftsman of any craft will be found in you any longer; and the sound of a mill will not be heard in you any longer;

The ultimate judgment is that there is no more music.

Part Two
Topical Concordance

EXPLANATION OF ENTRIES

Entries where the actual word appears in the references are set in bold face. When an idea or topic and not the actual word is used in a reference, the print will be in normal face (i.e., the word *accompaniment* appears in the text of Psalm 5:0; the idea or topic of accompaniment is suggested in Exodus 15:1, 1 Samuel 10:5, etc.).

Accompanied
2 Chronicles 5:13
2 Chronicles 29:27
Isaiah 5:12
see also **Accompaniment,** Accompaniment

Accompaniment
Psalm 5:0
see also **Accompanied,** Accompaniment

Accompaniment
Exodus 15:1
1 Samuel 10:5
Job 21:12
Psalm 12:0
Psalm 33:2, 3
Psalm 71:22
Psalm 92:3
Psalm 98:5, 6
Psalm 147:7
Psalm 149:3
Isaiah 23:16
Ezekiel 33:32
Revelation 5:8, 9
see also **Accompanied, Accompaniment**

Aijeleth Hashshahar
(the hind of the morning)
Psalm 22:0

Alamoth
(possibly *for soprano voices*)
1 Chronicles 15:20
Psalm 46:0

Al-tashheth
(do not destroy)
Psalm 57:0
Psalm 58:0
Psalm 59:0
Psalm 75:0

Amasai
1 Chronicles 15:24

Angels
Revelation 8:2—11:19

Asaph
1 Chronicles 6:39
1 Chronicles 15:19
1 Chronicles 16:5
1 Chronicles 25:1, 2, 6
2 Chronicles 5:12
2 Chronicles 29:30
2 Chronicles 35:15
Ezra 2:41

Ezra 3:10
Nehemiah 7:44
Nehemiah 11:22
Psalm 50:0
Psalm 73:0
Psalm 74:0
Psalm 75:0
Psalm 76:0
Psalm 77:0
Psalm 78:0
Psalm 79:0
Psalm 80:0
Psalm 81:0
Psalm 82:0
Psalm 83:0

Ascents
Psalm 120:0
Psalm 121:0
Psalm 122:0
Psalm 123:0
Psalm 124:0
Psalm 125:0
Psalm 126:0
Psalm 127:0
Psalm 128:0
Psalm 129:0
Psalm 130:0
Psalm 131:0
Psalm 132:0
Psalm 133:0
Psalm 134:0

Asharelah
1 Chronicles 25:2

Assembly
Exodus 15:1-21
Exodus 19:10-17
Exodus 20:18-21
Leviticus 23:36
Numbers 1-10
2 Chronicles 5:11-14
2 Chronicles 15:14
2 Chronicles 29:20-36
2 Chronicles 30:13-23
Psalm 68:24-27
Psalm 150:1-6

Jeremiah 4:5-8
Joel 1:2

Azarel
Nehemiah 12:36

Azaziah
1 Chronicles 15:21

Aziel
1 Chronicles 15:20

Bagpipe
Daniel 3:5
Daniel 3:7
Daniel 3:10
Daniel 3:15

Barak
Judges 4:6-5:31

Beating
Psalm 68:25
see also **Strike**

Benaiah
1 Chronicles 15:20, 24
1 Chronicles 16:5, 6

Blast
Exodus 19:13
Joshua 6:5
Hebrews 12:19

Blew
Joshua 6:8, 9, 16, 20
Judges 3:27
Judges 6:34
Judges 7:19, 20, 22
1 Samuel 13:3
2 Samuel 2:28
2 Samuel 18:16
2 Samuel 20:1, 22
1 Kings 1:39
2 Kings 9:13
2 Kings 11:14
1 Chronicles 15:24
1 Chronicles 16:6

Blew-Choir Director

2 Chronicles 7:6
2 Chronicles 13:14
2 Chronicles 23:13
see also **Blow, Blowing, Blown, Blows**

Blow
Numbers 10:5, 6, 7, 8, 10
Joshua 6:4, 9, 13
Judges 7:18
1 Kings 1:34
Psalm 81:3
Jeremiah 4:5
Jeremiah 6:1
Jeremiah 51:27
Ezekiel 33:6
Hosea 5:8
Joel 2:1
Zechariah 9:14
see also **Blew, Blowing, Blown, Blows**

Blowing
Leviticus 23:24
Numbers 29:1
Judges 7:20
2 Chronicles 5:12
see also **Blew, Blow, Blown, Blows**

Blown
Numbers 10:3, 4
Isaiah 18:3
Isaiah 27:13
Ezekiel 7:14
Amos 3:6
see also **Blew, Blow, Blowing, Blows**

Blows
Ezekiel 33:3
see also **Blew, Blow, Blowing, Blown**

Bugle
1 Corinthians 14:8

Bukkaiah
1 Chronicles 25:4

Castanets
2 Samuel 6:5

Celebration
Genesis 31:27
Exodus 15:1-21
Judges 5:1-31
Judges 11:34
2 Samuel 6:5-23
1 Kings 1:32-48
2 Kings 11:12-14
1 Chronicles 13:8
1 Chronicles 15:27-28
1 Chronicles 16:1-43
2 Chronicles 30:21
Nehemiah 12:27-47
Psalm 81:1-5
Isaiah 30:29
Luke 15:22-25

Chant
Ezekiel 32:16
see also **Chanted, Dirge, Lament**

Chanted
2 Samuel 1:17
2 Samuel 3:33
2 Chronicles 35:25
see also **Chant, Dirge, Lament**

Chenaniah
1 Chronicles 15:22

Choir
Nehemiah 12:38
Habakkuk 3:19

Choir Director
Psalm 4:0
Psalm 5:0
Psalm 6:0
Psalm 8:0
Psalm 9:0
Psalm 11:0
Psalm 12:0
Psalm 13:0
Psalm 14:0
Psalm 18:0

Choir Director-Dance

Psalm 19:0
Psalm 20:0
Psalm 21:0
Psalm 22:0
Psalm 31:0
Psalm 36:0
Psalm 39:0
Psalm 40:0
Psalm 41:0
Psalm 42:0
Psalm 44:0
Psalm 45:0
Psalm 46:0
Psalm 47:0
Psalm 49:0
Psalm 51:0
Psalm 52:0
Psalm 53:0
Psalm 54:0
Psalm 55:0
Psalm 56:0
Psalm 57:0
Psalm 58:0
Psalm 59:0
Psalm 60:0
Psalm 61:0
Psalm 62:0
Psalm 64:0
Psalm 65:0
Psalm 66:0
Psalm 67:0
Psalm 68:0
Psalm 69:0
Psalm 70:0
Psalm 75:0
Psalm 76:0
Psalm 77:0
Psalm 80:0
Psalm 81:0
Psalm 84:0
Psalm 85:0
Psalm 88:0
Psalm 109:0
Psalm 139:0
Psalm 140:0
Habakkuk 3:19

Choirs
Nehemiah 12:31–40

Clanging
1 Corinthians 13:1

Composed
Amos 6:5
see also Composition, **Psalmist**

Composition
Exodus 15:1
Deuteronomy 31:19–22
Deuteronomy 32:1–47
1 Samuel 18:6, 7
2 Samuel 1:17, 18
Psalm 33:3
Psalm 40:3
Psalm 98:1
Psalm 144:9
Song of Solomon 1:1
Isaiah 42:10–13
Amos 6:5
Revelation 5:9
Revelation 14:3
see also **Composed, Psalmist**

Cymbal
1 Corinthians 13:1
see also **Cymbals**

Cymbals
2 Samuel 6:5
1 Chronicles 13:8
1 Chronicles 15:16, 19, 28
1 Chronicles 16:5, 42
1 Chronicles 25:1
2 Chronicles 29:25
Ezra 3:10
Nehemiah 12:27
Psalm 150:5
see also **Cymbal**

Dance
Ecclesiastes 3:4
Song of Solomon 6:13
Jeremiah 31:13
Matthew 11:17

Dance-David

Luke 7:32
see also **Danced, Dances, Dancing**

Danced
Judges 21:23
1 Samuel 21:11
Matthew 14:6
Mark 6:22
see also **Dance, Dances, Dancing**

Dances
Judges 21:21
1 Samuel 29:5
Jeremiah 31:4
see also **Dance, Danced, Dancing**

Dancing
Exodus 15:20
Exodus 32:19
Judges 11:34
1 Samuel 18:6
1 Samuel 30:16
2 Samuel 6:14, 16
Psalm 30:11
Psalm 149:3
Psalm 150:4
Lamentations 5:15
Luke 15:25
see also **Dance, Danced, Dances**

David
1 Samuel 16:14-23
1 Samuel 18:10
1 Samuel 19:9
2 Samuel 1:17-27
2 Samuel 22:1-51
1 Chronicles 6:31
1 Chronicles 13:8
1 Chronicles 15:16, 27
1 Chronicles 25:1
2 Chronicles 7:6
2 Chronicles 29:25, 26, 27, 30
2 Chronicles 36:15
Ezra 3:10
Nehemiah 12:36, 45, 46
Psalm 3:0
Psalm 4:0
Psalm 5:0
Psalm 6:0
Psalm 7:0
Psalm 8:0
Psalm 9:0
Psalm 11:0
Psalm 12:0
Psalm 13:0
Psalm 14:0
Psalm 15:0
Psalm 16:0
Psalm 17:0
Psalm 18:0
Psalm 19:0
Psalm 20:0
Psalm 21:0
Psalm 22:0
Psalm 23:0
Psalm 24:0
Psalm 25:0
Psalm 26:0
Psalm 27:0
Psalm 28:0
Psalm 29:0
Psalm 30:0
Psalm 31:0
Psalm 32:0
Psalm 34:0
Psalm 35:0
Psalm 36:0
Psalm 37:0
Psalm 38:0
Psalm 39:0
Psalm 40:0
Psalm 41:0
Psalm 51:0
Psalm 52:0
Psalm 53:0
Psalm 54:0
Psalm 55:0
Psalm 56:0
Psalm 57:0
Psalm 58:0
Psalm 59:0
Psalm 60:0
Psalm 61:0
Psalm 62:0
Psalm 63:0
Psalm 64:0

Psalm 65:0
Psalm 68:0
Psalm 69:0
Psalm 70:0
Psalm 86:0
Psalm 101:0
Psalm 103:0
Psalm 108:0
Psalm 109:0
Psalm 110:0
Psalm 122:0
Psalm 124:0
Psalm 131:0
Psalm 133:0
Psalm 138:0
Psalm 139:0
Psalm 140:0
Psalm 141:0
Psalm 142:0
Psalm 143:0
Psalm 144:0
Psalm 145:0

Deborah
Judges 5:1-31

Dirge
Jeremiah 9:10, 20
Amos 5:1
Matthew 11:17
Luke 7:32
see also **Chant, Chanted, Lament**

Distinction
1 Corinthians 14:7

Dress
1 Chronicles 15:27
2 Chronicles 5:12
2 Chronicles 20:21
Ezra 3:10

Dynamics
Exodus 19:16, 19
Joshua 6:1-20
1 Kings 1:39-41
1 Chronicles 15:16, 28
2 Chronicles 30:21

Psalm 150:5
Ecclesiastes 12:4
Isaiah 42:11
Isaiah 58:1
Jeremiah 31:7
see also Sound quality

Eduth
Psalm 60:0
Psalm 80:0

Ehud
Judges 3:26-30

Eight-stringed
Psalm 6:0
Psalm 12:0
see also **Ten-stringed, Ten strings**

Elam
Nehemiah 12:42

Eleazar
Nehemiah 12:42

Eliab
1 Chronicles 15:20
1 Chronicles 16:5

Eliakim
Nehemiah 12:41

Eliashib
Ezra 10:24

Eliathah
1 Chronicles 25:4

Eliezer
1 Chronicles 15:24

Elioenai
Nehemiah 12:41

Eliphelehu
1 Chronicles 15:21

El Shoshannim-Flute

El Shoshannim
   Psalm 80:0

Emotions
   Genesis 31:27
   Exodus 19:16
   Exodus 20:18
   1 Samuel 18:6
   2 Samuel 1:17-27
   2 Samuel 3:31-39
   1 Kings 1:39-41
   1 Chronicles 16:33
   2 Chronicles 23:18
   2 Chronicles 29:30
   2 Chronicles 30:21
   2 Chronicles 35:25
   Nehemiah 12:27-47
   Job 21:12
   Job 29:13
   Job 38:7
   Job 39:24, 25
   Psalm 9:2
   Psalm 27:6
   Psalm 28:7
   Psalm 40:3
   Psalm 43:4
   Psalm 51:14
   Psalm 59:16, 17
   Psalm 65:13
   Psalm 67:4
   Psalm 71:22-24
   Psalm 77:6
   Psalm 81:1-3
   Psalm 87:7
   Psalm 92:4
   Psalm 95:1, 2
   Psalm 98:4-6, 8
   Psalm 100:1, 2, 4
   Psalm 138:2-4
   Psalm 149:5
   Proverbs 25:20
   Proverbs 29:6
   Ecclesiastes 3:4
   Isaiah 16:11
   Isaiah 24:8, 9
   Isaiah 30:29
   Isaiah 42:10, 11
   Isaiah 51:3
   Jeremiah 4:19
   Jeremiah 48:36
   Lamentations 5:15
   Ezekiel 7:14
   Amos 8:3, 10
   Matthew 11:17
   Luke 7:32
   Ephesians 5:19
   James 5:13

Ethan
   1 Kings 4:31
   1 Chronicles 15:19

Ethan the Ezrahite
   Psalm 89:0

Ezer
   Nehemiah 12:42

Figures of speech
   1 Chronicles 16:33
   Job 29:13
   Job 30:31
   Job 38:7
   Psalm 49:4
   Psalm 57:8
   Psalm 65:13
   Psalm 98:8
   Psalm 108:2
   Proverbs 25:20
   Isaiah 16:11
   Isaiah 23:14
   Isaiah 24:7, 8
   Isaiah 30:29
   Isaiah 42:11
   Isaiah 58:1
   Jeremiah 48:36
   Ezekiel 33:32
   Hosea 2:15
   Luke 7:32
   1 Corinthians 13:1
   Revelation 1:10
   Revelation 4:1
   Revelation 14:2

Flute
   1 Samuel 10:5

Flute-Harps

Job 21:12
Job 30:31
Psalm 5:0
Isaiah 5:12
Isaiah 30:29
Daniel 3:5, 7, 10, 15
Matthew 11:17
Luke 7:32
1 Corinthians 14:7
see also **Flute-players, Flutes**

Flute-players
Revelation 18:22
see also **Flute, Flutes**

Flutes
1 Kings 1:40
Psalm 87:7
Jeremiah 48:36
see also **Flute, Flute-players**

Gedaliah
1 Chronicles 25:3

Giddalti
1 Chronicles 25:4

Gilalai
Nehemiah 12:36

Gittith
Psalm 8:0
Psalm 81:0
Psalm 84:0

Gong
1 Corinthians 13:1

Hanani
1 Chronicles 25:4
Nehemiah 12:36

Hananiah
1 Chronicles 25:4
Nehemiah 12:41

Harp
1 Samuel 10:5

1 Samuel 16:16, 23
1 Samuel 18:10
1 Samuel 19:9
1 Chronicles 25:3
Job 21:12
Job 30:31
Psalm 33:2
Psalm 49:4
Psalm 57:8
Psalm 71:22
Psalm 81:2
Psalm 92:3
Psalm 108:2
Psalm 144:9
Psalm 150:3
Isaiah 5:12
Isaiah 16:11
Isaiah 23:16
Isaiah 24:8
Amos 6:5
1 Corinthians 14:7
Revelation 5:8
see also **Harpists, Harps**

Harpists
Revelation 14:2
Revelation 18:22
see also **Harp, Harps**

Harps
2 Samuel 6:5
1 Kings 10:12
1 Chronicles 13:8
1 Chronicles 15:16, 20, 28
1 Chronicles 16:5
1 Chronicles 25:1, 6
2 Chronicles 5:12
2 Chronicles 9:11
2 Chronicles 20:28
2 Chronicles 29:25
Nehemiah 12:27
Psalm 137:2
Isaiah 14:11
Ezekiel 26:13
Amos 5:23
Revelation 14:2
Revelation 15:2
see also **Harp, Harpists**

Hashabiah

1 Chronicles 25:3

Heman

1 Kings 4:31
1 Chronicles 6:33
1 Chronicles 15:19
1 Chronicles 16:42
1 Chronicles 25:1, 4-6
2 Chronicles 5:12
2 Chronicles 35:15

Heman the Ezrahite

Psalm 88:0

Higgaion Selah

Psalm 9:16
Psalm 92:3

Horn

Leviticus 25:9
Judges 3:27
1 Chronicles 15:28
Psalm 98:6
Daniel 3:5, 7, 10, 15
Hosea 5:8
see also **Horns**

Horns

2 Chronicles 15:14
Psalm 75:10
see also **Horn**

Hothir

1 Chronicles 25:4

Hymn

Matthew 26:30
Mark 14:26
see also **Hymns, Melody, Psalm, Psalms, Song, Songs, Taunt-song**

Hymns

Nehemiah 12:27, 46
Acts 16:25
Ephesians 5:19
Colossians 3:16
see also **Hymn, Melody, Psalm, Psalms, Song, Songs, Taunt-song**

Improvise

Amos 6:5
see also **Beating, Intones, Play, Played, Playing, Plays, Strike**

Indistinct

1 Corinthians 14:8

Instrument

Ezekiel 33:32
see also **Bagpipe, Bugle, Castanets, Cymbal, Cymbals, Flute, Flutes, Gong, Harp, Harps, Horn, Horns, Instruments, Lute, Lyre, Lyres, Pipe, Psaltery, Ram's horn, Ram's horns, Stringed instruments, Strings, Tambourine, Tambourines, Timbrel, Timbrels, Trigon, Trumpet, Trumpets**

Instrument construction
2 Samuel 6:5
1 Kings 10:12
1 Chronicles 23:5
2 Chronicles 9:11

Instruments

1 Samuel 18:6
2 Samuel 6:5
1 Chronicles 15:16
1 Chronicles 16:5, 42
1 Chronicles 23:5
2 Chronicles 5:13
2 Chronicles 7:6
2 Chronicles 23:13
2 Chronicles 29:26, 27
2 Chronicles 30:21
2 Chronicles 34:12
Nehemiah 12:36
Psalm 150:4
Isaiah 13:5
Isaiah 38:20
Habakkuk 3:19
see also **Bagpipe, Bugle, Castanets, Cymbal, Cymbals, Flute, Flutes, Gong, Harp, Harps, Horn, Horns,**

Instruments-Lament

Instrument, Lute, Lyre, Lyres, Pipe, Psaltery, Ram's horn, Ram's horns, Stringed instruments, Strings, Tambourine, Tambourines, Timbrel, Timbrels, Trigon, Trumpet, Trumpets

Intones
Isaiah 16:11
see also **Beating, Play, Played, Playing, Plays, Strike**

Jahath
2 Chronicles 34:12

Jahaziel
1 Chronicles 16:6

Jeduthun
1 Chronicles 16:42
1 Chronicles 25:6
2 Chronicles 5:12

Jeduthun
(Ethan the Ezrahite)
Psalm 39:0
Psalm 62:0
Psalm 77:0

Jehiah
1 Chronicles 15:24

Jehiel
1 Chronicles 15:20
1 Chronicles 16:5

Jehohanan
Nehemiah 12:42

Jeiel
1 Chronicles 15:21
1 Chronicles 16:5

Jeremiah
2 Chronicles 35:25

Jerimoth
1 Chronicles 25:4

Jeshaiah
1 Chronicles 25:3

Jezrahiah
Nehemiah 12:42

Joab
2 Samuel 2:28
2 Samuel 18:16
2 Samuel 20:22

Jonath Elem Rehokim
(probably *to the tune of "The Silent Dove in Far-off Lands"*)
Psalm 56:0

Joseph
1 Chronicles 25:2

Joshaphat
1 Chronicles 15:24

Joshbekashah
1 Chronicles 25:4

Jubal
Genesis 4:21

Judah
Nehemiah 12:36

Korah, sons of
Psalm 42:0
Psalm 44:0
Psalm 45:0
Psalm 46:0
Psalm 47:0
Psalm 48:0
Psalm 49:0
Psalm 84:0
Psalm 85:0
Psalm 87:0
Psalm 88:0

Lament
2 Samuel 1:17
2 Samuel 3:31, 33

Lament-Malchijah

2 Chronicles 35:25
see also **Chant, Chanted, Dirge**

Leadership
Exodus 15:1
Exodus 15:20, 21
1 Chronicles 6:31-48
1 Chronicles 9:33
1 Chronicles 15:16-29
1 Chronicles 16:1-43
1 Chronicles 25:1-31
2 Chronicles 23:18
2 Chronicles 34:12
Ezra 3:8-13
Nehemiah 11:22-24
Nehemiah 12:27-47
Habakkuk 3:19

Levites
1 Chronicles 9:33
2 Chronicles 30:21
2 Chronicles 34:12
2 Chronicles 35:15

Levites
1 Chronicles 6:31-48
1 Chronicles 13:1-6
1 Chronicles 15:16-29
1 Chronicles 16:1-43
1 Chronicles 25:1-31
2 Chronicles 5:11-14
2 Chronicles 6:4-7
2 Chronicles 23:16-21
Ezra 2:1-70
Ezra 3:8-13
Ezra 7:11-26
Nehemiah 12:27-47
Nehemiah 13:4-14

Loud-sounding
1 Chronicles 15:16, 28
1 Chronicles 16:5

Lute
Psalm 92:3

Lyre
Genesis 4:21
Genesis 31:27
1 Samuel 10:5
Psalm 33:2
Psalm 43:4
Psalm 57:8
Psalm 71:22
Psalm 81:2
Psalm 92:3
Psalm 98:5
Psalm 108:2
Psalm 147:7
Psalm 149:3
Psalm 150:3
Isaiah 5:12
Daniel 3:5, 7, 10, 15

Lyres
2 Samuel 6:5
1 Kings 10:12
1 Chronicles 13:8
1 Chronicles 15:16, 21, 28
1 Chronicles 16:5
1 Chronicles 26:1, 6
2 Chronicles 5:12
2 Chronicles 9:11
2 Chronicles 20:28
2 Chronicles 29:25
Nehemiah 12:27
Isaiah 30:32

Maai
Nehemiah 12:36

Maaseiah
1 Chronicles 15:20
Nehemiah 12:42

Mahalath
(sickness, a sad tone)
Psalm 53:0

Mahalath Leannoth
Psalm 88:0

Mahazioth
1 Chronicles 25:4

Malchijah
Nehemiah 12:42

Mallothi
1 Chronicles 25:4

Maskil
(possibly *contemplative* or *didactic* or *skillful psalm*)
Psalm 32:0
Psalm 42:0
Psalm 44:0
Psalm 45:0
Psalm 52:0
Psalm 53:0
Psalm 54:0
Psalm 55:0
Psalm 74:0
Psalm 78:0
Psalm 88:0
Psalm 89:0
Psalm 142:0

Mattaniah
1 Chronicles 25:4

Mattithiah
1 Chronicles 15:21
1 Chronicles 16:5
1 Chronicles 25:3

Melody
Psalm 98:5
Isaiah 51:3
Ephesians 5:19
see also **Hymn, Hymns, Psalm, Psalms, Song, Songs, Taunt-song**

Merari
2 Chronicles 34:12

Meshullam
2 Chronicles 34:12

Micaiah
Nehemiah 12:41

Mikhtam
(possibly *epigrammatic poem* or *atonement psalm*)
Psalm 16:0

Psalm 56:0
Psalm 57:0
Psalm 58:0
Psalm 59:0
Psalm 60:0

Mikneiah
1 Chronicles 15:21

Milalai
Nehemiah 12:36

Miniamin
Nehemiah 12:41

Minstrel
2 Kings 3:15

Moses
Exodus 15:1-21
Deuteronomy 31:19-22
Deuteronomy 32:1-43
Psalm 90:0
Revelation 15:3

Music
1 Chronicles 15:16
2 Chronicles 5:13
2 Chronicles 7:6
Psalm 92:3
Isaiah 30:32
Lamentations 5:14
Daniel 3:5, 7, 10, 15
Luke 15:25

Musical instruments
1 Samuel 18:6
1 Chronicles 16:5
2 Chronicles 23:13
2 Chronicles 29:26
2 Chronicles 34:12
Nehemiah 12:36

Musician
1 Samuel 16:18
see also **Musicians,** Musicians

Musicians-Playing

Musicians
Psalm 68:25
Revelation 18:22
see also **Musician,** Musicians

Musicians
see **Amasai,** Angels, **Asaph,
Asharelah, Azarel, Azaziah, Aziel,
Barak, Benaiah, Bukkiah,
Chenaniah, David, Deborah, Ehud,
Elam, Eleazar, Eliab, Eliakim,
Eliashib, Eliathah, Eliezer,
Elioenael, Eliphelehu, Ethan, Ezer,
Gedeliah, Giddalti, Gilalai,
Hanani, Hananiah, Hashabiah,
Heman, Hothir, Jahath, Jahaziel,
Jeduthun, Jehiah, Jehiel,
Jehohanan, Jeiel, Jeremiah,
Jerimoth, Jeshaiah, Jezrahiah,
Joab, Joseph, Joshaphat,
Joshbekashah, Jubal, Judah, Maai,
Maaseiah, Mahazioth, Malchijah,
Mallothi, Mattaniah, Mattithiah,
Merari, Meshullam, Micaiah,
Mikneiah, Milalai, Miniamin,
Moses, Nethanel, Nethaniah,
Obadiah, Obed-Edom, Romamti-
Ezer, Saul, Sheba, Shebaniah,
Shebuel, Shemaiah, Shemiramoth,
Shimei, Solomon, Unni, Uzzi,
Uzziel, Zaccur, Zechariah, Zeri**

Muth-labben
(death to the son)
Psalm 9:0

Nethanel
1 Chronicles 15:24
Nehemiah 12:36

Nethaniah
1 Chronicles 25:2

Noise
Amos 5:23

Noisy
1 Corinthians 13:1

Obadiah
2 Chronicles 34:12

Obed-edom
1 Chronicles 15:21, 24
1 Chronicles 16:5

Orchestra
1 Samuel 10:5
1 Chronicles 13:8
Nehemiah 12:27-47
Daniel 3:1-18

Pipe
Genesis 4:21
Psalm 150:4

Piping
Judges 5:16

Play
Genesis 4:21
1 Samuel 16:16, 17, 23
Psalm 33:3
Psalm 87:7
Isaiah 38:20
see also **Beating, Improvise,
Intones, Played, Player, Playing,
Plays, Pluck, Strike**

Played
1 Samuel 18:7
2 Kings 3:15
Matthew 11:17
Luke 7:32
1 Corinthians 14:7
see also **Beating, Improvise,
Intones, Play, Player, Playing,
Plays, Pluck, Strike**

Player
1 Samuel 16:16
see also **Beating, Improvise,
Intones, Play, Played, Playing,
Plays, Pluck, Strike**

Playing
1 Samuel 18:10

Playing-Praises

1 Samuel 19:9
1 Kings 1:40
see also **Beating, Improvise, Intones, Play, Played, Player, Plays, Pluck, Strike**

Plays
Ezekiel 33:32
see also **Beating, Improvise, Intones, Play, Played, Player, Playing, Pluck, Strike**

Pluck
Isaiah 23:16
see also **Beating, Improvise, Intones, Play, Played, Player, Playing, Plays, Strike**

Praise
Exodus 15:1-21
Judges 5:1-31
1 Chronicles 16:1-43
1 Chronicles 23:5
2 Chronicles 5:11-14
2 Chronicles 7:4-7
2 Chronicles 23:13
Ezra 3:10
Nehemiah 12:27-47
Psalm 7:17
Psalm 9:2
Psalm 21:13
Psalm 30:12
Psalm 40:3
Psalm 43:4
Psalm 61:8
Psalm 66:2
Psalm 69:30
Psalm 71:22
Psalm 104:33
Psalm 106:12
Psalm 135:3
Psalm 146:2
Psalm 147:1
Psalm 149:1, 3
Psalm 150:3-5
Isaiah 12:5
Jeremiah 20:13
Jeremiah 31:7
Acts 16:25
Romans 15:9
see also Praise, **Praised, Praises, Praising, Thanksgiving,** Thanksgiving

Praise
1 Chronicles 25:1-31
2 Chronicles 20:20-30
see also **Praise, Praised, Praises, Praising,** Thanksgiving

Praised
2 Chronicles 30:21
Ezra 3:11
see also **Praise,** Praise, **Praises, Praising, Thanksgiving,** Thanksgiving

Praises
2 Samuel 22:50
1 Chronicles 16:9
2 Chronicles 29:30
Psalm 9:11
Psalm 18:49
Psalm 27:6
Psalm 33:2
Psalm 47:6-7
Psalm 57:7, 9
Psalm 59:17
Psalm 66:4
Psalm 68:4, 32
Psalm 71:23
Psalm 75:9
Psalm 92:1
Psalm 98:4
Psalm 101:1
Psalm 105:2
Psalm 108:1, 3
Psalm 135:3
Psalm 138:1
Psalm 144:9
Psalm 146:2
Psalm 147:1, 7
Psalm 149:3
James 5:13
see also **Praise,** Praise, **Praised, Praising, Thanksgiving,** Thanksgiving

Praising-Psalm

Praising
1 Chronicles 23:5
1 Chronicles 25:3
2 Chronicles 20:22
Ezra 3:11
see also **Praise,** Praise, **Praised, Praises, Thanksgiving,** Thanksgiving

Priests
Joshua 6:1-21
2 Chronicles 5:11-14
2 Chronicles 7:4-7
2 Chronicles 30:21
Ezra 2:1-70
Ezra 3:8-13
Ezra 7:11-26
Nehemiah 12:27-47
Nehemiah 13:4-14

Prophesy
1 Samuel 10:1-13
2 Kings 3:13-20
1 Chronicles 25:1-31

Psalm
Psalm 3:0
Psalm 4:0
Psalm 5:0
Psalm 6:0
Psalm 8:0
Psalm 9:0
Psalm 11:0
Psalm 12:0
Psalm 13:0
Psalm 14:0
Psalm 15:0
Psalm 18:0
Psalm 19:0
Psalm 20:0
Psalm 21:0
Psalm 22:0
Psalm 23:0
Psalm 24:0
Psalm 25:0
Psalm 26:0
Psalm 27:0
Psalm 28:0
Psalm 29:0
Psalm 30:0
Psalm 31:0
Psalm 32:0
Psalm 34:0
Psalm 35:0
Psalm 36:0
Psalm 37:0
Psalm 38:0
Psalm 39:0
Psalm 40:0
Psalm 41:0
Psalm 46:0
Psalm 47:0, 7
Psalm 48:0
Psalm 49:0
Psalm 50:0
Psalm 51:0
Psalm 61:0
Psalm 62:0
Psalm 63:0
Psalm 64:0
Psalm 65:0
Psalm 66:0
Psalm 67:0
Psalm 68:0
Psalm 69:0
Psalm 70:0
Psalm 72:0
Psalm 73:0
Psalm 75:0
Psalm 76:0
Psalm 77:0
Psalm 79:0
Psalm 80:0
Psalm 81:0
Psalm 82:0
Psalm 83:0
Psalm 84:0
Psalm 85:0
Psalm 87:0
Psalm 88:0
Psalm 92:0
Psalm 98:0
Psalm 100:0
Psalm 101:0
Psalm 103:0
Psalm 108:0

Psalm-Selah

Psalm 109:0
Psalm 110:0
Psalm 138:0
Psalm 139:0
Psalm 140:0
Psalm 141:0
Psalm 143:0
Psalm 144:0
Psalm 145:0
Acts 13:33, 35
1 Corinthians 14:26
see also **Hymn, Hymns, Melody, Psalms, Song, Songs**

Psalmist
2 Samuel 23:1
see also **Composed,** Composition

Psalms
Psalm 95:2
Luke 20:42
Acts 1:20
Ephesians 5:19
Colossians 3:16
see also **Hymn, Hymns, Melody, Psalm, Song, Songs**

Psaltery
Daniel 3:5, 7, 10, 15

Ram's horn
Exodus 19:13
Leviticus 25:9

Ram's horns
Joshua 6:4, 6, 8, 13

Resounding
Psalm 92:3
Psalm 150:5

Romamti-Ezer
1 Chronicles 25:4

Sang
Exodus 15:1
Numbers 21:17
Judges 5:1
1 Samuel 18:7
2 Chronicles 20:21
2 Chronicles 29:28, 30
Ezra 3:11
Nehemiah 12:42
Job 38:7
Psalm 7:0
Psalm 106:12
Matthew 11:17
Luke 7:32
Revelation 5:9
Revelation 14:3
Revelation 15:3
see also **Sing, Singer, Singers, Singing, Sings, Sung**

Saul
1 Samuel 13:3

Selah
Psalm 3:2, 4, 8
Psalm 4:2, 4
Psalm 7:5
Psalm 9:16, 20
Psalm 20:3
Psalm 21:2
Psalm 24:6, 10
Psalm 32:4, 5, 7
Psalm 39:5, 11
Psalm 44:8
Psalm 46:3, 7, 11
Psalm 47:4
Psalm 48:8
Psalm 49:13, 15
Psalm 50:6
Psalm 52:3, 5
Psalm 54:3
Psalm 55:7, 19
Psalm 57:3, 6
Psalm 59:5, 13
Psalm 60:4
Psalm 61:4
Psalm 62:4, 8
Psalm 66:4, 7, 15
Psalm 67:1, 4
Psalm 68:7, 19, 32
Psalm 75:3
Psalm 76:3, 9

Selah-Sing

Psalm 77:3, 9, 15
Psalm 81:7
Psalm 82:2
Psalm 83:8
Psalm 84:4, 8
Psalm 85:2
Psalm 87:3, 6
Psalm 88:7, 10
Psalm 89:4, 37, 45, 48
Psalm 140:3, 5, 8
Psalm 143:6
Habakkuk 3:3, 9, 13

Sheba
2 Samuel 20:1

Shebaniah
1 Chronicles 15:24

Shebuel
1 Chronicles 25:4

Shemaiah
Nehemiah 12:36, 42

Sheminith
1 Chronicles 15:21

Shemiramoth
1 Chronicles 15:20
1 Chronicles 16:5

Shiggaion
(dithyrambic rhythm or wild, passionate song)
Psalm 7:0

Shimei
1 Chronicles 25:3

Shoshannim
(lilies)
Psalm 45:0
Psalm 69:0

Shushan Eduth
(the lily of testimony)
Psalm 60:0
see also **Signal**

Signal
2 Chronicles 13:4-12
Jeremiah 51:27
see also Signal

Signal
Exodus 19:16
Leviticus 25:9
Numbers 31:6
Joshua 6:1-21
Judges 3:27
Judges 7:1-25
1 Samuel 13:3
2 Samuel 2:28
2 Samuel 15:10
2 Samuel 18:16
2 Samuel 20:1
2 Samuel 20:22
1 Kings 1:32-48
2 Kings 9:13
Nehemiah 4:20
Isaiah 5:1
Isaiah 27:13
Jeremiah 4:5, 19
Jeremiah 6:1, 17
Ezekiel 33:3-6
Daniel 3:1-18
Hosea 5:8
Hosea 8:1
Joel 2:1, 15
Matthew 6:2
Matthew 24:31
1 Corinthians 14:7, 8
1 Corinthians 15:52
1 Thessalonians 4:16
see also **Signal**

Sing
Exodus 15:1, 21
Numbers 21:17
Judges 5:3, 10, 12
1 Samuel 21:11
1 Samuel 29:5
2 Samuel 22:50
1 Chronicles 16:9, 33
1 Chronicles 25:6
2 Chronicles 29:30
Job 21:12

Sing-Singing

Job 29:13
Job 33:27
Psalm 7:17
Psalm 9:2, 11
Psalm 13:6
Psalm 18:49
Psalm 21:13
Psalm 27:6
Psalm 30:4, 12
Psalm 33:1-3
Psalm 47:6, 7
Psalm 51:14
Psalm 57:7, 9
Psalm 59:16, 17
Psalm 61:8
Psalm 65:13
Psalm 66:2, 4
Psalm 67:4
Psalm 68:4, 32
Psalm 71:22, 23
Psalm 75:9
Psalm 81:1
Psalm 87:7
Psalm 89:1
Psalm 92:1, 4
Psalm 95:1
Psalm 96:1, 2
Psalm 98:1, 4, 5
Psalm 101:1
Psalm 104:33
Psalm 105:2
Psalm 108:1, 3
Psalm 135:3
Psalm 137:3, 4
Psalm 138:1, 5
Psalm 144:9
Psalm 146:2
Psalm 147:1, 7
Psalm 149:1, 3, 5
Ecclesiastes 12:4
Isaiah 5:1
Isaiah 23:16
Isaiah 27:2
Isaiah 42:10, 11
Jeremiah 20:13
Jeremiah 31:7
Hosea 2:15
Zephaniah 2:14

Zechariah 2:10
Romans 15:9
1 Corinthians 14:15
Hebrews 2:12
James 5:13
see also **Sang, Singer, Singers, Singing, Sings, Sung**

Singer
1 Chronicles 6:33
see also **Sang, Sing, Singers, Singing, Sings, Sung**

Singers
1 Kings 10:12
1 Chronicles 9:33
1 Chronicles 15:16, 19, 27
2 Chronicles 5:12, 13
2 Chronicles 9:11
2 Chronicles 23:13
2 Chronicles 29:28
2 Chronicles 35:15, 25
Ezra 2:41, 70
Ezra 7:7, 24
Ezra 10:24
Nehemiah 7:1, 44, 67, 73
Nehemiah 10:28, 39
Nehemiah 11:22
Nehemiah 12:28, 29, 42, 45, 46, 47
Nehemiah 13:5, 10
Psalm 68:25
Ecclesiastes 2:8
Ezekiel 40:44
see also **Sang, Sing, Singer, Singing, Sings, Sung**

Singing
Exodus 32:18
1 Samuel 18:6
2 Samuel 19:35
1 Chronicles 15:22, 27
1 Chronicles 25:7
2 Chronicles 20:22
2 Chronicles 23:18
Ezra 2:65
Psalm 100:2
Psalm 107:22
Matthew 26:30

147

Singing-Song

Mark 14:26
Acts 16:25
Ephesians 5:19
Colossians 3:16
see also **Sang, Sing, Singer, Singers, Sings, Sung**

Sings
Proverbs 25:20
Proverbs 29:6
see also **Sang, Sing, Singer, Singers, Singing, Sung**

Skill
Psalm 137:5
see also Skill, **Skillful, Skillfully**

Skill
Nehemiah 10:28
Ezekiel 33:32
see also **Skill, Skillful, Skillfully**

Skillful
1 Samuel 16:16, 18
1 Chronicles 15:22
1 Chronicles 25:7
2 Chronicles 34:12
Psalm 47:7
see also **Skill,** Skill, **Skillfully**

Skillfully
Psalm 33:3
Isaiah 23:16
see also **Skill,** Skill, **Skillful**

Soloist
Deuteronomy 32:1-43
Judges 11:34
1 Samuel 13:3
1 Samuel 16:14-23
1 Samuel 18:10
1 Samuel 19:9
2 Samuel 18:16
2 Samuel 20:1-22
2 Samuel 22:1-51

Solomon
Nehemiah 12:45

Psalm 72:0
Psalm 127:0
Song of Solomon 1:1

Song
Exodus 15:1, 2
Numbers 21:17
Deuteronomy 31:19, 21, 22, 30
Deuteronomy 32:44
Judges 5:12
2 Samuel 1:18
2 Samuel 22:1
1 Chronicles 6:31, 32
2 Chronicles 29:27
Psalm 18:0
Psalm 28:7
Psalm 30:0
Psalm 33:3
Psalm 40:3
Psalm 42:8
Psalm 45:0
Psalm 46:0
Psalm 48:0
Psalm 65:0
Psalm 66:0
Psalm 67:0
Psalm 68:0
Psalm 69:12, 30
Psalm 75:0
Psalm 76:0
Psalm 77:6
Psalm 81:2
Psalm 83:0
Psalm 87:0
Psalm 88:0
Psalm 92:0
Psalm 96:1
Psalm 98:1
Psalm 108:0
Psalm 118:14
Psalm 120:0
Psalm 121:0
Psalm 122:0
Psalm 123:0
Psalm 124:0
Psalm 125:0
Psalm 126:0
Psalm 127:0

Song-Sound

Psalm 128:0
Psalm 129:0
Psalm 130:0
Psalm 131:0
Psalm 132:0
Psalm 133:0
Psalm 134:0
Psalm 137:4
Psalm 144:9
Psalm 149:1
Ecclesiastes 7:5
Ecclesiastes 12:4
Song of Solomon 1:1
Isaiah 5:1
Isaiah 12:2, 5
Isaiah 23:15
Isaiah 24:9
Isaiah 26:1
Isaiah 42:10
Lamentations 3:14, 63
Ezekiel 33:32
Revelation 5:9
Revelation 14:3
Revelation 15:3
see also **Hymn, Hymns, Melody, Psalm, Psalms, Songs**

Song leaders
Nehemiah 11:23

Songs
Genesis 31:27
1 Kings 4:32
1 Chronicles 13:8
1 Chronicles 16:42
Nehemiah 12:8, 27
Job 35:10
Psalm 32:7
Psalm 78:63
Psalm 119:54
Psalm 137:3
Proverbs 25:20
Song of Solomon 1:1
Isaiah 23:16
Isaiah 24:16
Isaiah 30:29
Isaiah 38:20
Ezekiel 26:13

Amos 5:23
Amos 6:5
Amos 8:3, 10
Ephesians 5:19
Colossians 3:16
see also **Hymn, Hymns, Melody, Psalm, Psalms, Song**

Song text
Exodus 15:1-21
Numbers 21:17
Deuteronomy 32:1-43
Judges 5:1-31
1 Samuel 18:7
1 Samuel 21:11
1 Samuel 29:5
2 Samuel 1:17-27
2 Samuel 3:33-34
2 Samuel 22:1-51
2 Samuel 23:1-7
1 Chronicles 16:8-36
Ezra 3:10-11
Psalms
Song of Solomon
Isaiah 5:1-30
Isaiah 26:1-6
Habakkuk
Revelation 5:9-10
Revelation 15:3-4

Sound
Exodus 19:16, 19
Exodus 20:18
Exodus 32:18
Leviticus 25:9
Numbers 10:9
Joshua 6:5, 20
2 Samuel 6:15
2 Samuel 15:10
1 Kings 1:41
1 Chronicles 15:19, 28
1 Chronicles 16:42
2 Chronicles 13:12
Nehemiah 4:20
Job 21:12
Psalm 47:5
Psalm 98:5, 6
Psalm 150:3

Sound-Tambourines

Isaiah 30:29
Isaiah 51:3
Jeremiah 4:19, 21
Jeremiah 6:17
Jeremiah 42:14
Ezekiel 26:13
Ezekiel 33:4, 5
Daniel 3:5, 7, 10, 15
Hosea 5:8
Joel 2:1
Amos 2:2
Amos 5:23
Amos 6:5
Matthew 6:2
1 Corinthians 14:7-8
1 Corinthians 15:52
Revelation 1:10
Revelation 4:1
Revelation 8:6, 13
Revelation 10:7
Revelation 14:2
Revelation 18:22
see also **Sounded, Sounding, Sounds**

Sounded
2 Chronicles 29:28
Revelation 8:7, 8, 10, 12
Revelation 9:1, 13
Revelation 11:15
see also **Sound, Sounding, Sounds**

Sounding
Numbers 10:7
Psalm 81:2
see also **Sound, Sounded, Sounds**

Sound quality
see **Blast, Clanging, Distinction, Indistinct, Loud-sounding, Noise, Noisy, Resounding, Sweet, Unison, Voice, Wails**

Sounds
Exodus 19:13
1 Chronicles 15:16
Job 39:25
see also **Sound, Sounded, Sounding**

Strike
Psalm 81:2
see also **Beating, Improvise, Intones, Play, Played, Player, Playing, Plays, Pluck**

Stringed instruments
Psalm 4:0
Psalm 6:0
Psalm 45:8
Psalm 54:0
Psalm 55:0
Psalm 61:0
Psalm 67:0
Psalm 76:0
Psalm 150:4
Isaiah 38:20
Habakkuk 3:19

Strings
Psalm 33:2
Psalm 144:9
Isaiah 23:16

Sung
Job 36:24
Isaiah 26:1
see also **Sang, Sing, Singer, Singers, Singing, Sings**

Support
Ezra 7:24
Nehemiah 10:34-39
Nehemiah 12:44-47
Nehemiah 13:4-14

Sweet
2 Samuel 23:1
Psalm 81:2

Tambourine
1 Samuel 10:5
Isaiah 5:12
see also **Tambourines**

Tambourines
Judges 11:34
1 Samuel 18:6

Tambourines-Therapy

2 Samuel 6:5
1 Chronicles 13:8
Psalm 68:25
Isaiah 24:8
Isaiah 30:32
Jeremiah 31:4
see also **Tambourine**

Taunt-song
Habakkuk 2:6

Teaching
Deuteronomy 31:19-22
2 Samuel 1:18
1 Chronicles 15:22
1 Chronicles 25:1-31
Colossians 3:16

Temple
2 Kings 12:13

Ten-stringed
Psalm 92:3
see also **Eight-stringed, Ten strings**

Ten strings
Psalm 33:2
Psalm 144:9
see also **Eight-stringed, Ten-stringed**

Terms
see **Aijeleth Hashshahar, Alamoth, Al-tashheth, Ascents, Gittith, Higgaion Selah, Jonath Elem Rehokim, Mahalath, Mahalath Leannoth, Maskil, Mikhtam, Muth-labben, Selah, Sheminith, Shiggaion, Shoshannim, Shushan Eduth**

Thank
1 Chronicles 16:4
Psalm 28:7
see also **Thankfulness, Thanks, Thanksgiving,** Thanksgiving

Thankfulness
Colossians 3:16
see also **Thank, Thanks, Thanksgiving,** Thanksgiving

Thanks
2 Samuel 22:50
1 Chronicles 25:3
2 Chronicles 20:21
Ezra 3:11
Psalm 7:17
Psalm 18:49
Psalm 30:4, 12
Psalm 33:2
Psalm 57:9
Psalm 92:1
Psalm 108:3
Psalm 138:1
see also **Thanks, Thankfulness, Thanksgiving,** Thanksgiving

Thanksgiving
Nehemiah 12:8
Nehemiah 12:27, 46
Psalm 69:30
Psalm 95:2
Psalm 107:22
Psalm 147:7
Isaiah 51:3
see also **Thank, Thankfulness, Thanks,** Thanksgiving

Thanksgiving
2 Samuel 22:1-51
1 Chronicles 16:1-43
Ezra 3:10, 11
Nehemiah 12:27-47
Psalm 13:6
Psalm 33:2, 3
Psalm 57:7-9
Psalm 108:1-3
see also **Praise,** Praise, **Praised, Praises, Praising**

Therapy
1 Samuel 16:14-23
1 Samuel 18:10-11
1 Samuel 19:9-10

151

Timbrel-Trumpets

Timbrel
Genesis 31:27
Exodus 15:20
Job 21:12
Psalm 81:2
Psalm 149:3
Psalm 150:4
see also **Timbrels**

Timbrels
Exodus 15:20
see also **Timbrel**

Trigon
Daniel 3:5, 7, 10, 15

Trumpet
Exodus 19:16, 19
Exodus 20:18
Joshua 6:5, 20
Judges 6:34
Judges 7:18
1 Samuel 13:3
2 Samuel 2:28
2 Samuel 6:15
2 Samuel 15:10
2 Samuel 18:16
2 Samuel 20:1, 22
1 Kings 1:34, 39, 41
2 Kings 9:13
Nehemiah 4:20
Job 39:24, 25
Psalm 47:5
Psalm 81:3
Psalm 150:3
Isaiah 18:3
Isaiah 27:13
Isaiah 58:1
Jeremiah 4:5, 19, 21
Jeremiah 6:1, 17
Jeremiah 42:14
Jeremiah 49:2
Jeremiah 51:27
Ezekiel 7:14
Ezekiel 33:3-6
Hosea 5:8
Hosea 8:1
Joel 2:1, 15
Amos 2:2
Amos 3:6
Zephaniah 1:16
Zechariah 9:14
Matthew 6:2
Matthew 24:31
1 Corinthians 15:52
1 Thessalonians 4:16
Hebrews 12:19
Revelation 1:10
Revelation 4:1
Revelation 8:13
Revelation 9:14
see also **Trumpets**

Trumpeter
Nehemiah 4:18
see also **Trumpeters**

Trumpeters
2 Kings 11:14
2 Chronicles 5:13
2 Chronicles 23:13
Revelation 18:22
see also **Trumpeter**

Trumpets
Leviticus 23:24
Numbers 10:2, 8-10
Numbers 29:1
Numbers 31:6
Joshua 6:4, 6, 8, 9, 13, 16, 20
Judges 7:8, 16, 18-20, 22
2 Kings 11:14
2 Kings 12:13
1 Chronicles 13:8
1 Chronicles 15:24, 28
1 Chronicles 16:6, 42
2 Chronicles 5:12, 13
2 Chronicles 7:6
2 Chronicles 13:12, 14
2 Chronicles 15:14
2 Chronicles 20:28
2 Chronicles 23:13
2 Chronicles 29:26-28
Ezra 3:10
Nehemiah 12:35, 41
Psalm 98:6

Revelation 8:2, 6
see also **Trumpet**

Tuned
1 Chronicles 15:20-21

Unison
2 Chronicles 5:13

Unni
1 Chronicles 15:20

Uzzi
Nehemiah 12:42

Uzziel
1 Chronicles 25:4

Voice
Job 39:24

Wails
Jeremiah 48:36

War
  Exodus 15:1-21
  Numbers 10:1-10
  Numbers 31:1-12
  Joshua 6:1-21
  Judges 3:26-30
  2 Chronicles 13:14
  Job 39:24, 25
  Isaiah 30:27-33
  Isaiah 38:10-20
  Jeremiah 4:19-22

Warnings
  Exodus 32:18, 19
  Job 21:12, 13
  Isaiah 5:11, 12
  Isaiah 23:16
  Amos 5:23
  Amos 6:5

Witness
  Deuteronomy 31:19-22
  Joshua 6:1-21
  Psalm 9:11
  Psalm 40:3
  Psalm 51:14
  Psalm 57:7, 9
  Psalm 59:16, 17
  Psalm 66:2, 4
  Psalm 67:4
  Psalm 68:4
  Psalm 69:30
  Psalm 75:9, 10
  Psalm 89:1
  Psalm 92:1-4
  Psalm 96:1, 2
  Psalm 98:1
  Psalm 137:2-4
  Psalm 138:5
  Psalm 149:1, 5
  Isaiah 12:1-6

Women
  Exodus 15:20, 21
  Judges 5:1-31
  1 Samuel 18:6-9
  2 Samuel 19:35
  Ezra 2:65
  Nehemiah 7:67
  Psalm 68:25
  Ecclesiastes 2:8
  Ecclesiastes 12:4

Worship
  Psalm 66:4
  Isaiah 27:13
  Daniel 3:5, 10, 15
  see also Worship

Worship
  Exodus 32:18
  Nehemiah 12:27-47
  1 Corinthians 14:26
  see also **Worship**

Worshiped
  2 Chronicles 29:30
  Daniel 3:7

Zaccur
  1 Chronicles 25:2

Zechariah-Zeri

Zechariah
1 Chronicles 15:20, 24
1 Chronicles 16:5
2 Chronicles 34:12
Nehemiah 12:41

Zeri
1 Chronicles 25:3

Hebrew Concordance

Abar: 5674a, to pass over, through or by, pass on
Leviticus 25:9

Anah: 6031b, to sing
Exodus 32:18
Numbers 21:17
1 Samuel 18:7
1 Samuel 21:11
1 Samuel 29:5
Ezra 3:11
Psalm 147:7
Isaiah 27:2
Hosea 2:15

Asor: 6218, a ten, decade
Psalm 33:2
Psalm 92:3
Psalm 144:9

Bin: 995, to discern
1 Chronicles 15:22
1 Chronicles 25:7
2 Chronicles 34:12

Chagag: 2287, to make a pilgrimage, keep a pilgrimage feast
1 Samuel 30:16

Chalil: 2485, flute, pipe
1 Samuel 10:5
1 Kings 1:40
Isaiah 5:12
Isaiah 30:29
Jeremiah 48:36

Chalal: 2490b, to play the pipe, to pipe
1 Kings 1:40
Psalm 87:7

Chashab: 2803, to think, account
Amos 6:5

Chatsar: 2690, to sound a trumpet
1 Chronicles 15:24
1 Chronicles 16:6
2 Chronicles 5:12
2 Chronicles 7:6
2 Chronicles 13:14
2 Chornicles 29:28

Chatsotsrah: 2689, trumpet
Numbers 10:2, 8, 9, 10
Numbers 31:6
2 Kings 11:14
2 Kings 12:13
1 Chronicles 13:8
1 Chronicles 15:24, 28
1 Chronicles 16:6, 42
2 Chronicles 5:12, 13
2 Chronicles 7:6
2 Chronicles 13:12, 14
2 Chronicles 15:14
2 Chronicles 20:28
2 Chronicles 23:13
2 Chronicles 29:26, 27, 28
Ezra 3:10
Nehemiah 12:35, 41
Psalm 96:8
Hosea 5:8

Chul: 2342a, to whirl, dance, writhe
Judges 21:23

Dabar: 1696, to speak
Judges 5:12

Debar: 1697, speech, word
Psalm 137:3

Echad: 259, one
2 Chronicles 5:13

Gal: 7032a, voice
Daniel 3:5, 7, 10, 15

Halal: 1984b, to be boastful, to praise
1 Chronicles 23:5

2 Chronicles 23:13
2 Chronicles 29:30
2 Chronicles 30:21
Ezra 3:10, 11
Psalm 69:30
Psalm 78:63
Psalm 135:3
Psalm 146:2
Psalm 147:1
Psalm 149:1, 3
Psalm 150:3, 4, 5
Jeremiah 20:13
Jeremiah 31:7

Hamah: 1993, to murmur, growl, roar, be boisterous
Isaiah 16:11
Jeremiah 48:36

Hamon: 1995, a sound, murmur, roar, crowd, abundance
Ezekiel 26:13
Amos 5:23

Hemjah: 1998, a sound, music
Isaiah 14:11

Higgaion Selah: 1902, resounding music, meditation, musing
Psalm 9:16
Psalm 92:3

Huyyedoth: 1960, songs of praise
Nehemiah 12:8

Karar: 3769, to dance
2 Samuel 6:14, 16

Keli: 3627, an article, utensil, vessel
Ezekiel 33:32
1 Chronicles 15:16
1 Chronicles 16:5, 42
1 Chronicles 23:5
2 Chronicles 5:13
2 Chronicles 7:6
2 Chronicles 23:13
2 Chronicles 29:26, 27
2 Chronicles 30:21

2 Chronicles 34:12
Nehemiah 12:36

Kinnor: 3658, a lyre
Genesis 4:21
Genesis 31:27
1 Samuel 10:5
1 Samuel 16:16, 23
2 Samuel 6:5
1 Kings 10:12
1 Chronicles 13:8
1 Chronicles 15:16, 21, 28
1 Chronicles 16:5
1 Chronicles 25:1, 3, 6
2 Chronicles 5:12
2 Chronicles 9:11
2 Chronicles 20:28
2 Chronicles 29:25
Nehemiah 12:27
Job 21:12
Job 30:31
Psalm 33:2
Psalm 43:4
Psalm 49:4
Psalm 57:8
Psalm 71:22
Psalm 81:2
Psalm 92:3
Psalm 98:5
Psalm 108:2
Psalm 137:2
Psalm 149:3
Psalm 150:3
Isaiah 5:12
Isaiah 16:11
Isaiah 23:16
Isaiah 24:8
Isaiah 30:32
Ezekiel 26:13

Machol: 4234, a dance (masculine)
Jeremiah 31:4, 13
Psalm 30:11
Psalm 149:3
Psalm 150:4
Lamentations 5:15

Manginah: 4485, (mocking, derisive) song
Lamentations 3:63

Mashak: 4900, to draw, drag
Exodus 19:13
Joshua 6:5
Job 39:25

Mashal: 4912, a proverb, parable
Habbakkuk 2:6

Mashroqi: 4953, a (musical) pipe
Daniel 3: 5, 7, 10, 15

Maskil: 4905b, a contemplative poem
Psalm 47:7

Massa: 4853a, a load, burden, lifting, bearing tribute
1 Chronicles 15:22, 27

Mecholah: 4246, a dance (feminine)
Exodus 15:20
Exodus 32:19
Judges 11:34
Judges 21:21
1 Samuel 18:6
1 Samuel 21:11
1 Samuel 29:5
Song of Songs 6:13

Men: 4482a, string (of a harp)
Psalm 45:8
Psalm 150:4

Menaanea: 4517, (a kind of musical) rattle—castanets
2 Samuel 6:5

Metsiltayim: 4700, cymbals
1 Chronicles 13:8
1 Chronicles 15:16, 19, 28
1 Chronicles 16:5, 42
1 Chronicles 25:1, 6
2 Chronicles 5:12, 13
2 Chronicles 29:25

Ezra 3:10
Nehemiah 12:27

Nagan: 5059, to touch or play a stringed instrument
1 Samuel 16:16, 17, 18, 23
1 Samuel 18:10
1 Samuel 19:9
2 Kings 3:15
Psalm 33:3
Psalm 68:25
Isaiah 23:16
Isaiah 38:20
Ezekiel 33:32

Naim: 5273b, singing, sweetly sounding, musical
2 Samuel 23:1
Psalm 81:2

Natsach: 5329, preeminent or enduring
Habakkuk 3:19

Nebel: 5035b, a harp or a lute, guitar
1 Samuel 10:5
2 Samuel 6:5
1 Kings 10:12
1 Chronicles 13:8
1 Chronicles 15:16, 20, 28
1 Chronicles 16:5
1 Chronicles 25:1, 6
2 Chronicles 5:12
2 Chronicles 9:11
2 Chronicles 20:28
2 Chronicles 29:25
Nehemiah 12:27
Psalm 33:2
Psalm 57:8
Psalm 71:22
Psalm 81:2
Psalm 92:3
Psalm 108:2
Psalm 144:9
Psalm 150:3
Isaiah 5:12
Isaiah 14:11
Amos 6:5
Amos 5:23

Hebrew Concordance

Neginah: 5058, music
Psalm 69:12
Psalm 77:6
Isaiah 38:20
Lamentations 3:14
Lamentations 5:14
Habakkuk 3:19

Parat: 6527, perhaps divide
Amos 6:5

Peh: 6310, mouth
Amos 6:5

Pesanterin: 6460, perhaps a trigon
Daniel 3:5, 7, 10, 15

Qeren: 7161, a horn
Psalm 75:10

Qeren: 7162, a horn
Daniel 3:5, 7, 10, 15

Qitharos: 7030, a lyre, zither
Daniel 3:5, 7, 10, 15

Qol: 6963, sound, voice
Exodus 19:16, 19
Exodus 20:18
Exodus 32:18
Joshua 6:5, 20
2 Samuel 6:15
2 Samuel 15:10
1 Chronicles 15:10, 19, 28
1 Kings 1:41
Nehemiah 4:20
Job 21:12
Job 39:24
Psalm 47:5
Psalm 98:5, 6
Isaiah 51:3
Jeremiah 4:19, 21
Jeremiah 6:17
Jeremiah 42:14
Ezekiel 26:13
Ezekiel 33:4, 5
Amos 2:2

Qonen: 6969, to chant an elegy or dirge
2 Samuel 1:17
2 Samuel 3:33
2 Chronicles 35:25
Ezekiel 32:16

Ranan: 7442, to give a ringing cry
1 Chronicles 16:33
Job 29:13
Job 38:7
Psalm 5:11
Psalm 20:5
Psalm 33:1
Psalm 51:14
Psalm 59:16
Psalm 63:7
Psalm 67:4
Psalm 81:1
Psalm 84:2
Psalm 90:14
Psalm 92:4
Psalm 95:1
Psalm 96:12
Psalm 98:4, 8
Psalm 132:9, 16
Psalm 149:5
Proverbs 29:6
Isaiah 42:11
Jeremiah 31:7
Zechariah 2:10

Raqad: 7540, to skip about
Ecclesiastes 3:4

Renanah: 7445, a ringing cry
Psalm 100:2

Rinnab: 7440, a ringing cry
2 Chronicles 20:22
Psalm 107:22

Ron: 7438, a ringing cry
Psalm 32:7

Rua: 7321, to raise a shout, give a blast
Numbers 10:7, 9
2 Chronicles 13:12

Hosea 5:8
Joel 2:1

Sabbeka: 5443, trigon
Daniel 3:5, 7, 10, 15

Sachaq: 7832, to laugh
1 Samuel 18:7

Shalish: 7991b, perhaps a sistrum
1 Samuel 18:6

Shama: 8085, to hear
1 Chronicles 15:16, 19, 28
1 Chronicles 16:5, 42
Nehemiah 12:42

Shir: 7891, to sing
Exodus 15:1, 21
Judges 5:3
1 Samuel 18:6
2 Samuel 19:35
1 Kings 10:12
1 Chronicles 6:33
1 Chronicles 9:33
1 Chronicles 15:16, 19, 27
1 Chronicles 16:9, 33
2 Chronicles 5:12, 13
2 Chronicles 9:11
2 Chronicles 23:13
2 Chronicles 35:15, 25
Ezra 2:41, 65, 70
Ezra 7:7
Ezra 10:24
Nehemiah 7:1, 44, 67, 73
Nehemiah 10:28, 39
Nehemiah 11:22, 23
Nehemiah 12:28, 29, 42, 45, 46, 47
Nehemiah 13:5, 10
Job 33:27
Job 36:24
Psalm 13:6
Psalm 21:13
Psalm 27:6
Psalm 33:3
Psalm 57:7
Psalm 59:16
Psalm 65:13

Psalm 68:4, 25, 32
Psalm 87:7
Psalm 89:1
Psalm 96:1, 2
Psalm 98:1
Psalm 101:1
Psalm 104:33
Psalm 105:2
Psalm 108:1
Psalm 137:3, 4
Psalm 138:5
Psalm 144:9
Psalm 149:1
Proverbs 25:20
Ecclesiastes 2:8
Ecclesiastes 12:4
Isaiah 5:1
Isaiah 26:1
Isaiah 42:10
Jeremiah 20:13
Ezekiel 40:44
Zephaniah 2:14

Shir: 7892a, song
Genesis 31:27
Exodus 15:1
Numbers 21:17
Judges 5:1, 12
1 Kings 4:32
1 Chronicles 6:31, 32
1 Chronicles 13:8
1 Chronicles 15:16
1 Chronicles 16:42
1 Chronicles 25:6, 7
2 Chronicles 5:13
2 Chronicles 7:6
2 Chronicles 20:21
2 Chronicles 23:13
2 Chronicles 29:27, 28
2 Chronicles 34:12
Nehemiah 12:27, 36, 46
Psalm 28:7
Psalm 33:3
Psalm 40:3
Psalm 42:8
Psalm 69:30
Psalm 96:1
Psalm 98:1

Psalm 106:12
Psalm 137:3, 4
Psalm 144:9
Psalm 149:1
Proverbs 25:20
Ecclesiastes 7:5
Ecclesiastes 12:4
Song of Songs 1:1
Isaiah 23:16
Isaiah 24:9
Isaiah 26:1
Isaiah 30:29
Ezekiel 26:13
Ezekiel 33:32
Amos 5:23
Amos 6:5
Amos 8:10

Shirah: 7892b, song
Genesis 31:27
Exodus 15:1
Numbers 21:17
Deuteronomy 31:19, 21, 22, 30
Deuteronomy 32:44
2 Samuel 22:1
Isaiah 5:1
Isaiah 23:15
Amos 8:3

Shofar: 7782, a horn (for blowing)
Exodus 19:16, 19
Exodus 20:18
Leviticus 25:9
Joshua 6:4, 5, 6, 8, 9, 13, 16, 20
Judges 3:27
Judges 6:34
Judges 7:8, 16, 18, 19, 20, 22
1 Samuel 13:3
2 Samuel 2:28
2 Samuel 6:15
2 Samuel 15:10
2 Samuel 18:16
2 Samuel 20:1
1 Kings 1:34, 39, 41
2 Kings 9:13
1 Chronicles 15:28
2 Chronicles 15:14
Nehemiah 4:20

Job 39:24, 25
Psalm 47:5
Psalm 81:3
Psalm 98:6
Psalm 150:3
Isaiah 18:3
Isaiah 27:13
Isaiah 58:1
Jeremiah 4:5, 19, 21
Jeremiah 6:1, 17
Jeremiah 42:14
Jeremiah 51:27
Ezekiel 33:3, 4, 5, 6
Hosea 8:1
Joel 2:1, 15
Amos 2:2
Amos 3:6
Zephaniah 1:16
Zephaniah 9:14

Siach: 7878, to muse, complain, talk
Judges 5:10

Sumponeyah: 5481, a bagpipe
(siphoneya, Arabic)
Daniel 3:5, 7, 10, 15

Taphaph: 8608, to sound the timbrel, beat
Psalm 68:25

Taphas: 8610, to lay hold of, wield
Genesis 4:21

Taqa: 8628, to thrust, clap, give a blow, blast
Numbers 10:3, 4, 5, 6, 7, 8, 10
Joshua 6:4, 8, 9, 13, 16, 20
Judges 3:27
Judges 7:18, 19, 20, 22
1 Samuel 13:3
2 Samuel 2:28
2 Samuel 18:16
2 Samuel 20:1, 22
1 Kings 1:34, 39
2 Kings 9:13
2 Kings 11:14
2 Chronicles 23:13

Taqa-Zamar

Psalm 81:3
Isaiah 18:3
Isaiah 27:13
Jeremiah 4:5
Jeremiah 6:1
Jeremiah 51:27
Ezekiel 3:33
Ezekiel 7:14
Ezekiel 33:6
Hosea 5:8
Joel 2:1, 15
Amos 3:6
Zechariah 9:14

Taqoa: 8619, a blast or wind instrument
Ezekiel 7:14

Tehillah: 8416, praise, song of praise
Psalm 40:3
Psalm 66:2
Psalm 106:12
Psalm 147:1
Psalm 149:1

Teruah: 8643, a shout or blast of war, alarm, or joy
Leviticus 23:24
Numbers 29:1
Psalm 150:5
Jeremiah 49:2

Todah: 8426, thanksgiving
Nehemiah 12:27, 31, 38, 40

Toph: 8596, a timbrel, tambourine
Genesis 31:27
Exodus 15:20
Judges 11:34
1 Samuel 10:5
1 Samuel 18:6
2 Samuel 6:5
1 Chronicles 13:8
Job 21:12
Psalm 68:25
Psalm 81:2
Psalm 149:3
Psalm 150:4
Isaiah 5:12

Isaiah 24:8
Isaiah 30:32
Jeremiah 31:4

Tsanteroth: 6804, pipes
Judges 5:16

Tseltselim: 6767d, cymbal
2 Samuel 6:5
Psalm 150:5

Uggab: 5748: a flute
Genesis 4:21
Job 21:12
Job 30:31
Psalm 150:4

Yada: 3045, to know
1 Samuel 16:16, 18

Yadah: 3034, to throw, cast
Nehemiah 12:46
Psalm 43:4
Psalm 71:22

Yatab: 3190, to be good, well, glad, or pleasing
Psalm 33:3
Psalm 137:5
Isaiah 23:16

Yobel: 3104, a ram, a ram's horn
Exodus 19:13
Joshua 6:4, 6, 8, 13

Zamar: 2167, to make music
Judges 5:3
2 Samuel 22:50
1 Chronicles 16:9
Psalm 7:17
Psalm 9:2, 11
Psalm 18:49
Psalm 21:13
Psalm 27:6
Psalm 30:4, 12
Psalm 33:2
Psalm 47:6, 7
Psalm 57:7, 9

Psalm 59:17
Psalm 61:8
Psalm 66:2, 4
Psalm 68:4, 32
Psalm 71:22, 23
Psalm 75:9
Psalm 92:1
Psalm 98:4, 5
Psalm 101:1
Psalm 104:33
Psalm 105:2
Psalm 108:1, 3
Psalm 135:3
Psalm 138:1
Psalm 144:9
Psalm 146:2
Psalm 147:1, 7
Psalm 149:3
Isaiah 12:5

Zamir: 2158, song
2 Samuel 23:1
Job 35:10
Psalm 95:2
Psalm 119:54
Isaiah 24:16
Isaiah 25:5

Zemar: 2170, music
Daniel 3:5, 7, 10, 15

Zimrah: 2172, melody, song
Exodus 15:2
Psalm 81:2
Psalm 98:5
Psalm 118:14
Isaiah 51:3

Zimrath: 2176, melody, song
Isaiah 12:2

Greek Concordance

Ado: 103, to sing
Ephesians 5:19
Colossians 3:16
Revelation 5:9
Revelation 14:3
Revelation 15:3

Alalazo: 214, to raise a war cry
1 Corinthians 14:1

Auleo: 832, to play on a flute
Matthew 11:17
Luke 7:32
1 Corinthians 14:7

Auletos: 834, a flute player
Matthew 9:23
Revelation 18:22

Aulos: 836, a pipe, flute
1 Corinthians 14:7

Chalkos: 5475, copper or bronze
1 Corinthians 13:1

Choros: 5525, a dance
Luke 15:25

Echeo: 2278, to make a loud noise, to sound
1 Corinthians 13:1

Echos: 2279, a noise, sound
Hebrews 12:19

Exomologeo: 1843, to agree, confess
Romans 15:9

Humneo: 5214, to sing, to laud
Matthew 26:14
Matthew 26:30
Mark 14:26
Acts 16:25
Hebrews 2:12

Humnos: 5215, a hymn
Ephesians 5:19
Colossians 3:16

Kithara: 2788, a lyre
1 Corinthians 14:7
Revelation 5:8
Revelation 14:2
Revelation 15:2

Kitharizo: 2789, to play on a lyre
1 Corinthians 14:7

Kitharodos: 2790, (a singer) one who plays and sings to the lyre
Revelation 14:2
Revelation 18:22

Kumbalom: 2950, cymbal
1 Corinthians 13:1

Mousikos: 3451, skilled in the arts
Revelation 18:22

Ode: 5603, a song, ode
Ephesians 5:19
Colossians 3:16
Revelation 5:9
Revelation 14:3
Revelation 15:3

Orcheomai: 3738, to dance
Matthew 11:17
Matthew 14:6
Mark 6:22
Luke 7:32

Phone: 5456, a voice
Revelation 14:2
Revelation 18:22

Psallo: 5567, (to rub) to pull, twitch, twang, play, sing
Romans 15:9

Greek Concordance

1 Corinthians 14:15
Ephesians 5:19
James 5:13

Psalmos: 5568, a striking, a psalm
Luke 20:42
Luke 24:44
Acts 1:20
Acts 13:33, 35
1 Corinthians 14:26
Ephesians 5:19
Colossians 3:16

Salpigx: 4536, a trumpet
Matthew 24:31
1 Corinthians 14:8
1 Corinthians 15:52
1 Thessalonians 4:16
Hebrews 12:19
Revelation 1:10
Revelation 4:1
Revelation 8:8, 6, 13
Revelation 9:14

Salpistes: 4538, a trumpeter
Revelation 18:22

Salpizo: 4537, to sound a trumpet
Matthew 6:2
1 Corinthians 15:52
Revelation 8:6, 7, 8, 10, 12
Revelation 9:1, 13
Revelation 10:7
Revelation 11:15

Sumphonia: 4858, symphony, music
Luke 15:25

Threneo: 2354, to lament
Matthew 11:17
Luke 7:32

Notes

Notes

Notes

Notes

Also available from Cornerstone Press Chicago

The Responsibility of the Christian Musician
by Glenn Kaiser

Music charms the savage beast and brings mad kings into quiescence; it can also divide households and split churches. Few are more in touch with the problems and the solutions than Glenn Kaiser, lead singer for REZ and an inner-city pastor for more than twenty-five years. Young people in every era have tended to live in the "me, here, and now." In this book, Glenn makes an appeal for them to expand their sense of responsibility in God beyond just themselves to their family, church, and community at large. Helpful for parents and pastors as well as young music lovers and musicians.
ISBN 0-940895-21-8 • 75 pages $6.75

More Like the Master: A Christian Musician's Reader
Edited by Pat Peterson & Jane Hertenstein

A thought-provoking collection of articles and essays by Glenn Kaiser, Michael Card, Charlie Peacock, Dwight Ozard, Jan Krist, John Thompson, Michael Hakanson-Stacy, and Jeremy Begbie. Topics range from music as mission, the art and calling of music ministry, and how to deal with (or not deal with) record labels. Engaging chapters for musicians and ministers alike.
ISBN 0-940895-25-0 • 140 pages • $8.45

Description		Qty.	Amount

All orders must be prepaid. Checks (U. S. funds only) should be made payable to Cornerstone Press Chicago.	Subtotal	
__ Check enclosed __ MasterCard __ VISA	Shipping	
	Total	

Account number _____

Signature _____ Exp. date _____

Name _____

Address _____

City _____ State ____ Zip _____

Daytime phone _____
(required for credit card orders)

Send order to:
Cornerstone Press Chicago
939 W. Wilson Ave.
Chicago, IL 60640

or call, toll-free:
1-888-40-PRESS